AIRBNB INVESTING 101
BECOME A SUPERHOST, REPLACE THE 9-5 AND JOIN THE NEW RICH

JAMES BETT

LUCKY BOOK PUBLISHING

Become a Superhost
Replace the 9-5
and Join the New Rich

JAMES BETT

LUCKY BOOK PUBLISHING

Copyright © 2022 James Bett
All rights reserved. No part of this book may be reproduced or used in any manner without the prior written permission of the copyright owner, except for the use of brief quotations in a book review.
To request permissions, contact the publisher at
hello@luckybookpublishing.com.
First paperback edition October 2022.
LuckyBookPublishing.com/airbnb

Real estate investing, even on a very small scale, remains a tried and true means of building an individual's cash flow and wealth.

- Robert Kiyosaki

CONTENTS

Acknowledgments	ix
Introduction	xi
CHAPTER 1 - THE PROFITABLE AIRBNB	1
Analyzing Your Airbnb Investment	8
The Metrics that Matter	14
Valuing Your Airbnb Investment	17
Ask Yourself	19
CHAPTER 2 - FURNISH TO IMPRESS	20
Understanding Airbnb Demographics	22
Impressing The Different Guest Types	27
Ask Yourself	37
CHAPTER 3 - P IS FOR PRICE	38
The maximum fill rate approach	41
The maximum rate per night approach	42
The long-term approach	43
The combination approach	44
Ask Yourself	52
CHAPTER 4 - THE TRIPLE FACTOR	53
The Pictures	54
The Title	61
The Description	65
Ask Yourself	68
CHAPTER 5 - SUCCESSFUL HOSTING	69
Your Response Rate	71
Marketing Techniques	76
Five-Star Reviews	80
Ask Yourself	86

CHAPTER 6 - AUTOPILOT MANAGEMENT	87
What should I automate?	90
Automation Strategy	102
Ask Yourself	103
CHAPTER 7 - AIRBNBING WITHOUT PROPERTY	104
Rental Arbitrage	105
Co-Hosting	112
Airbnb Consultant	113
STR Property Manager	115
Airbnb Cleaning Service	118
Airbnb Superhost Ambassador	120
Ask Yourself	121
CHAPTER 8 - MITIGATE RISKS	122
Legal / Regulatory Concerns for Airbnb Properties	124
Insurance	129
Low Season Risks	134
Ask Yourself	138
CLOSING	139
RESOURCES	141
AUTHORS NOTE	143
BONUS CONTENT: CHECKLISTS AND TEMPLATES	145

ACKNOWLEDGMENTS

I dedicate this book to my amazing little family and community.

To my wife, Jessica. You are the beautiful rainbow in our family's pot of gold. You keep everything in our household running as we make all the sacrifices to make our dreams come true. I love you.

To our beautiful children. Words truly cannot explain how much I love you. All our sacrifices now are so mommy and daddy can always be there for all of you. You have our whole hearts.

To the Airbnb Hosting community. Thank you for opening your homes to me and sharing your courageous conversations. You are business owners and neighbors and serve our world. You survived the pandemic and are superheroes in our community. Bravo Zulu.

To our amazing publishing team, Samantha and Simar. Thank you for believing in me and helping to bring my story to life so we can help tens of thousands of people and their families achieve freedom through Airbnb investing.

Together we are better.

- James Bett

As a reader of this book you can get the book resources (Airbnb checklists and templates) for free at
www.luckybookpublishing.com/Airbnb

INTRODUCTION

Jamie has a great Airbnb business going. She quit her job a couple years ago and now travels, exploring the world. She isn't staying in five-star hotels or eating at Michelin restaurants, but that never appealed to her.

In fact, the last time I heard from Jamie she was with her German friend on an archaeological dig, uncovering Roman mosaics along the Mediterranean coast in southern Turkey.

Her Instagram looks like the Lonely Planet blog.

Adrian also has a great Airbnb business going. He schedules a few guests a year, not too many, just enough to pay for his yearly vacations and Christmas shopping. He likes his life in north London, his friends, his job, his family, but he also wants to be able to follow his passion for scuba diving around the world and to donate his time to unpaid charity work.

Maybe you've been "doing Airbnb" for a while now, and you're still working toward your goal. Maybe you want to be financially free to quit your day job and travel or work on independent projects, and you wonder what it takes to get there.

Or maybe you just want enough worry-free income to add some extras to your life.

Or hey, maybe you're crushing it with Airbnb and looking to expand your horizons.

Wherever you are, this book is for you. I've achieved the freedom and success I wanted with Airbnb, which is like anything else--you get out of it what you put into it, and it sure helps to have someone with years of successful experience guide you along the way. You CAN become a Superhost.

It's work, like anything worthwhile in life, but the payoff can be incredible. My experience is that virtually anybody currently doing Airbnb can be doing better, no matter what level they're at today.

The fact that you've read this far means you believe it, too.

So for those of you just starting out, congratulations on having what it takes to step out and follow your dream! I'm going to give you information I wish I had starting out so I would not have made nearly as many mistakes. I would not have wasted nearly as much time, and I would have been freed from the daily grind a lot sooner.

And for you experienced hands looking to take your Airbnb dreams to the next level, I'll give you crucial information to help accomplish your goal of scaling your business according to tried and true plans.

Both beginners and experts follow the same principles. First-time stock market investors and Warren Buffett are both looking to buy low and sell high. Six-year olds picking up a tennis racket for the first time and Rafael Nadal are both told by their coach to keep their eye on the ball.

Whether you're new to this whole Airbnb thing or if you've been at it for years, you're reading this book because you know you can be doing better, and you want the voice of experience to help you without wasting your time on Google to solve the problem. You're making, or are about to make, a serious investment in Airbnb. I'm here to help you ensure as much as possible that your investment pays off, and you have the choice to quit your 9 to 5 and join the new rich.

Like Jamie, you may want Airbnb to free you from the demands of a daily job so you can travel and follow your passion in life. Or like Adrian, you may want a nice reliable little side hustle to provide you with a second income while staying rooted in your community.

I've made my share of mistakes --I'm ashamed to tell you how long it was before I had proper pictures up instead of just phone shots, what a disaster my pricing plan was the first year, all those wonderful guest reviews I wasted and how much it cost me to think I didn't need professional advice for insurance. I do. You do.

And believe me, I am NEVER AGAIN accepting a New Year's Eve booking from guests I don't personally know! My neighbors still helpfully remind me about it.

It took me years to earn the knowledge in this book. Hopefully, it'll only take you a weekend of careful, intentional reading. You will still make your share of mistakes, we all do, but hey, they give you great stories!

You're in good hands. Let's get started.

CHAPTER 1 - THE PROFITABLE AIRBNB

> **KEY TAKEAWAY:**
> This chapter addresses the key investment metrics and other important considerations you should be able to answer when choosing an Airbnb investment property - or whether to turn your primary residence into one.

No matter what level of Airbnb hosting you're at, if you're reading this book that means you have some important questions:

"How much (more) income can I earn from the investment property?"

"How much will it cost?"

"Will it be worth the work and hassle?"

"What are the hidden expenses I could run into?"

"Am I making the right decision?"

No doubt you have other questions, and you should. Getting into this business at all, or expanding your commitment to short-term rental (STR) properties, is a serious investment decision not to be taken lightly.

This chapter will introduce you to the basic Airbnb investing concepts to set you up for success.

The Three Airbnb Markets

There are basically three main types of Airbnb markets. They can overlap with each other, but your property will fall primarily into one of these. There isn't a "wrong" or a "right" market; all types will come with a combination of volatility, stability, and revenue.

No matter which one you're in, *it is absolutely crucial that you understand the fundamental market type* of a certain location, as this guides you into how you should go about pricing, attracting guests, planning for expansion, etc.

As Avery Carl says in the very helpful book *Short-Term Rental, Long-Term Wealth*, "A random strategy yields random results." Treating a metro market STR as if you're next door to a fantastically popular tourist destination like Disneyland is not a recipe for success.

But for any and all of these markets, the same fundamentals apply. You will need to become familiar with things like average occupancy rate, nightly rates, the monthly mortgage you're paying if applicable, fixed costs such as electric and water, monthly property fees (including any homeowner association covenants or regulations) and more. We'll go over these later in the chapter.

1. Metro markets

What They Are:

Here we're talking New York City, Paris, San Francisco, London, Rome, etc. These are big places where tourism is not the primary industry. Generally there's more risk for STRs with metro markets, since there are usually a lot more regulations to worry about, so you must do the research to understand the regulations as they will be much more strict than in more tourist-oriented places.

Regulations covering Airbnb and other STR ventures are currently in a state of flux in most metro markets. STRs are a relatively new presence, so many localities are still grappling with how to regulate them, and they can change--sometimes significantly--from year to year, so make sure your research is up to date.

Why are things so dicey in big cities, where you'd figure Airbnb would be the most welcome? The hotel industry is taking the challenge of STRs seriously and is doing everything it can to limit the number of STRs available in large metropolitan areas. While this does limit the number of Airbnb properties in the lucrative big city market, those who do survive can really cash in. May this be you if you're in a metro market, but please, do the research to make sure you *fully* understand the regulatory hurdles you face. You may even consider hiring a property lawyer to help, it could save you a lot of time and grief.

The Pros:

Airbnb was born in San Francisco, a metro market. These markets have been very profitable for Airbnb investors. STR properties can generate cash quickly since occupancy rates are not as dependent on seasonal variables as other locations, and, quite simply, a lot of people pass through big cities.

The Cons:

As we've said, the regulatory deck is stacked against STRs in the metro areas, not to mention disgruntled neighbors, who are far more prevalent in big cities than in regional or national vacation destinations. The reputation of STRs as freewheeling bachelor party pads or as busy nuisances have prompted local homeowners and residents to take a few isolated incidents and present them to their local government as if they're the norm, which they're not, to try to regulate STRs out of existence. That's the world metro region STRs are in right now.

2. Regional vacation markets

What They Are:

Regional vacation markets are generally smaller towns, such as Branson, Missouri, Wisconsin Dells, Atlantic City, Big Bear Lake in California, Vermont during leaf season and other places that wouldn't show up on the map if it were not for their tourism.

These are places known for being vacation destinations where short-term visitors are their lifeblood. Airbnbs and other STRs here don't have the adversarial relationship with local governments, hotel industry lobbyists and neighbors that STRs have in metro markets -- far from it, regional vacation markets want to do everything they can to increase accommodation units in their area.

People in these places get it, they know they need tourism to survive, so they're much more willing to use STRs to boost the local economy than freeze them out. Their calculus is More Accommodation Space = More Tourists = More Income For All = More Government Revenue.

The tourism industry mindset which dominates regional vacation markets is very different from the travel industry dominating metro markets. The tourism mindset sees accommodation as one necessary ingredient in the whole recipe of profitability. The travel mindset sees accommodation as the whole ball game, a zero-sum equation where every dollar spent on an STR could have gone to a hotel that pays the government more in taxes than STRs do.

And since metro markets are far less reliant on tourism than regional vacation markets, they're far more likely to severely restrict STRs.

The Pros:

Local government is your friend in regional vacation markets. Short-term vacation rentals of cabins and private homes are an accepted way of life here; and regional vacation markets view STRs as a welcome feature, never as a threat. They want you to succeed and the local government does everything it can to help you.

Regional vacation markets typically have stability. In fact, many STR experts would rate regional vacation markets as the best places for STRs when balancing income (which is generally higher in metro markets) against the relaxed, friendly, headache-free regulation in regional vacation markets. Investments in STRs here are generally as stable as STRs get, although not always as profitable.

The Cons:

You probably won't get quite the cash flow here as you would in the metro markets and you're usually more seasonally dependent. Regional vacation markets are more of a long-term investment than a quick money venture.

3. National vacation markets

These are the high-profile, bucket list destinations -- Disney World, Niagara Falls, New Orleans, Maui, Las Vegas, the places everybody thinks of when it comes time for a holiday. A general rule: you drive to a regional vacation market; you fly to a national vacation market. The latter are bigger and more seasonally stable than regional vacation markets, but rely on tourism much more than metro markets do.

STRs are part of the landscape in these places and have been for a long time, which is both good and bad.

The Pros:

Zoning regulations are already established. Government policies won't pull the rug out from under your feet one day and shut you down like they're constantly trying to do in metro markets. When things are good economically and people are looking for ways to spend cash, STRs around national vacation markets do well.

The Cons:

Regulation, while well-established and predictable, is strict. There isn't much prime STR growth in these areas, and national vacation markets with significant permanent residential populations -- known as "voters" to local governments -- usually tightly restrict STRs to certain neighborhoods. And when things are tight economically, national vacation markets are the first to feel the downturn.

ANALYZING YOUR AIRBNB INVESTMENT

So when it comes to analyzing the profitability of your Airbnb, in addition to which of the three Airbnb markets most closely fits your property, there are certain factors you must consider:

Location

This is the central, most important consideration. If you're on Pitcairn Island, please contact me for a full refund, as nothing in this book will help you. Which one of the three markets above do you fall into? Does that mean you need to attract more business or leisure travelers? This is actually a quite fluid category. Consult the latest AirDNA (http://www.airdna.co) forecast to stay up to date.

- Overall, of course, STRs in well-traveled tourist locations generate more income, although STRs near smaller and mid-sized cities and resort areas are picking up in popularity. If you want to expand an STR business, that's a great way to go. But if you're just into renting out your existing home, you're tied to maximizing where you are.
- In general, if you're trying to appeal to tourists, you'll want a place convenient to public transportation and as many touristy attractions as possible. Walking distance to restaurants, shops and nightlife is another positive factor. We'll discuss key furnishing, listing and hosting considerations for tourist-oriented STRs later in the book.
- Check existing Airbnb listings to see if a certain location is oversaturated, underserved or just right for expansion. If you think it's underserved, be

careful, since there might be a reason for that. As the old business saying goes, if there are no shoe stores in a town, this is either a great place to open a shoe store or there's a reason there's no shoe store here already. Check the local area carefully if you find an unusually low number of STRs. What you would ideally like to see is a modest but growing number of STRs with occupancy rates over 50% near a regional or national vacation market.

Demand

The good news is that demand for STRs overall is increasing -- a lot. But so is the supply to meet that demand. Listings were up 15% from 2021 to 2022 according to AirDNA, keeping pace with what they calculate as a 14% increase in demand.

- Occupancy is about 60%, compared to 53.7% in 2019 (let's not even talk about the Covid years, shall we?), with overall revenues and the Average Daily Rate (ADR) growing as well. In fact, according to AirDNA, the Revenue Available Per Room (RevPAR) has increased from $114.26 in 2019 to $149.41.

Property

If you're mainly attracting business travelers, particularly if you're in a metro market, your guests will probably prefer a smaller property with a unique twist they don't get in the hotels they're tired of (which is why they're searching out your STR). They'll be more impressed with professionalism delivered with a zing -- "local color" is NEVER an excuse for a shoddy or sloppy property or service.

- If you're in a vacation area there will be more demand for family-sized homes, no matter if it's actually a family booking the property. Couples staying somewhere for a few days generally prefer larger homes, two or three-bedroom, even though it's just the two of them.
- How much work does the property need to either get ready for occupancy or to maintain? We'll discuss this later, but one major mistake many people make jumping into the STR business is neglecting to factor in how much time and energy they're going to spend, and whether it will be worth it or not.
- What's your unique flair? People are searching you out because they don't want to stay in a generic hotel. What will catch their eye, interest them in your property? Whatever you can do to stand out is to your advantage. We'll go over this in more detail later in the book.
- Protip: Get to know millennials and understand what they want. They're by far the most likely to search out a different, unique travel experience, preferring an unusual Airbnb to a soulless national chain hotel.

Seasonality

Common sense rules here. If you're on North Carolina's Outer Banks, the winter is not going to be your maximum income-generating time. If you're in Whistler, B.C., summer is your slow season.

- Some STR owners prefer a property that is highly seasonal, so they can live in it during the off-season and recoup their investment when things get busy.

Occupancy

"Occupancy" is quite simple; it's just the nights your property was rented divided by the nights it was available. Pretty basic math. Some properties can cover their yearly operating expenses with a month's occupancy, while others need more than that.

- Figure what your occupancy needs to be given your overhead (fixed) expenses and your income goals. For some properties, the Average Length of Stay (ALOS) will be higher than for others -- national vacation markets vs. metro markets, for example. Can you afford to absorb the loss during the slow season?
- And bear in mind that while the nightly rental price is almost always higher for short-term stays than the long-term's nightly price, high turnover also means higher expenses (see below).
- A property that allows more guests to stay at once is a property that, over time, gets booked more often.

Revenue

Times are good for STRs these days -- AirDNA reports that across the board STRs listed as full-time saw annual average revenues of $56,000 in 2021. That's the highest ever recorded, and as people get back to traveling there's every reason to expect it to increase.

- For your property you can calculate your Average Daily Rate (ADR), which is your gross take divided by the number of days it was rented.

Expenses

You have to have a clear understanding of how much you're forking out each month to maintain your property. And we're not just talking about financial outlays, but time, energy and mindshare.

- Be sure to count booking fees paid to Airbnb, all fixed utilities, property taxes, mortgages, etc.
- Do not underestimate cleaning costs. The more turnover the higher these will be -- seven guests staying two nights each is more expensive than one guest staying fourteen nights because you need to do a lot more room cleaning.
- Figure in the things you have to upgrade or replace like soap, towels, sheets, kitchen items, coffee, everything.
- Remember to count your own time as an expense. If you're handling all the booking and billing yourself, how much time is that going to demand? How far do you live from the property? Are you planning on doing all the maintenance and upkeep yourself, or are you hiring a property management company? Will you need to be on call 24/7? Can you afford the mindshare running an STR property will require?

Ongoing Research

Part of your work is keeping up with the data. Fortunately there are plenty of sites pulling together the important numbers for you. I've used the following sites and can recommend them, and there are no doubt other good ones out there:

- Airbtics (www.airbtics.com)
- Rabbu (www.rabbu.com)
- AllTheRooms (www.alltherooms.com)
- BeyondPricing (www.beyondpricing.com)
- AirDNA (www.airdna.co)

THE METRICS THAT MATTER

There are six investment metrics that Airbnb investors need to look out for:

Occupancy rate

Obviously one of the fundamentals. But we're not talking about just the raw number of guests you have booked, but the number of guests booked against the total number of nights it was available for occupancy throughout the year. Your occupancy pretty much determines your rate of return, your income and your cash flow, all the reasons you're in this business to begin with.

- Occupancy is a function of, primarily, location. Yep, there it is. If you're looking to invest in Airbnb as a business or to expand your existing Airbnb operation, you've got a lot more leeway in location than if you're just trying to let out your existing home. Still, there are things you can do if you can't do anything about your location to boost your occupancy rate.
- By far the most important thing you can do to maximize occupancy in a given location is to capitalize on positive guest reviews. Good guest reviews are gold mines. They significantly -- significantly -- influence your occupancy. One recent study on Mashvisor found that in San Francisco, a city with one of the highest STR occupancy rates anywhere, "the number of reviews has a 27% influence on occupancy rates," making it the single most important factor within a given location. Other high-occupancy locations figure guest reviews count anywhere from 25% to 34% towards occupancy rates.

- Maximize guest reviews by featuring them prominently on your site. Guests are far more likely to book with a property that garners great reviews than they are to go with a place they haven't heard anything good about. After all, wouldn't you be?
- If you know a guest has had a positive experience at your property, incentivize them to leave a review by offering them a discount on a future stay, or gift certificates.

Airbnb rental income

Again, just so we're clear, this is not gross income. Gross income of $50,000 a year looks great for a property with yearly expenses of $5,000, the Airbnb rental income there is $45,000. But if your outlay is $45,000 then your rental income is $5,000.

- Your **Airbnb cash flow** is simple to figure, it's your monthly income minus your monthly expenses. $1,000 a month income - $300 a month expenses = $700 a month cash flow. Not rocket science.
- Your **capitalization rate** is your net cash flow per month times 12 months. If you're looking at purchasing a property, you need to know if the cap rate is good. Calculate it by dividing the property price by net operating income. If your monthly cash flow is $700, that's $8,400 a year in net operating income.
- **Cash on cash return** is simply doing the same thing but dividing net operating income by what money you paid out of pocket, which includes investment property financing. Obviously there are more

complicated factors involved when totaling out of pocket expenses than we can detail here, you may want to consult a property finance professional.
- Word to the wise: Don't skimp on hiring professional services when you really need them. It's a false economy. This is one of the biggest mistakes I made. The #1 thing I would do over if I were starting out again is to pay for a *lot* more professional advice early on. You can't know and do everything equally well yourself. If you're a professional photographer, you don't have to pay someone to do your site pictures; if you're not a professional, you're losing money by not hiring a pro to take the pictures since your property invariably looks amateurish with amateur photos and who wants that?
- Same with your insurance, and maybe with interior decorating and marketing or even a real estate advisor. Professionals exist because, used judiciously, they can add more value than what you're paying them. So if you're not sure that the numbers are falling in your favor for your Airbnb investment, set up an appointment with a financial advisor who can bring much-needed clarity.

Airbnb return on investment

You are now in a good position to determine if you can reasonably expect to make enough of a return on your Airbnb investment to make it worth your time. You're answering the basic question: will the return be worth the cost, time and effort?"

VALUING YOUR AIRBNB INVESTMENT

The importance of understanding a property's value can't be overstated. This is one area where you may consider paying for professional advice, since pros can see things you can't and will bring up considerations you haven't thought of.

Still, you can get a pretty good rough idea of what you're looking at with the five following strategies condensed from Investopedia, which I've found useful when applied to STRs:

1. **The Sales Comparison Approach.** This is what your local real estate agent or appraiser is most likely to use when evaluating a property. Basically, you simply compare what similar homes in your area have sold or rented for in the past several months, or whatever time frame gives you an accurate picture. Taken into account, of course, are such factors as a property's bedrooms, bathrooms, garage, swimming pool, pizza oven, decks, etc.
2. **The Capital Asset Pricing Model.** This is a more comprehensive look. It includes the potential return on investment (ROI) you might expect from rental income and compares it to other investment opportunities -- in short, what else you could do with that money. It figures the risk factors of your particular rental property, as they can vary widely even within the same area. CAPM, as Investopedia says, "helps you determine what return you deserve for putting your money at risk."
3. **The Income Approach.** This is a popular metric for commercial real estate investing, it looks at how much you can expect to receive for rental property

yields relative to your initial investment. This model involves a lot of assumptions and some sophisticated financial presuppositions, but essentially it tries to determine what you're going to earn in annual income compared to the current value of the property with all considerations taken into account.

4. **Gross Rent Multiplier Approach.** This "values a rental property based on the amount of rent an investor can collect each year," according to Investopedia. It's quick, it's easy, but it doesn't take into account costs like taxes, utilities, insurance or other very real expenses. GRM is a number to throw in the mix; it's not the whole picture.

5. **The Cost Approach.** This is really more used to value vacant land, as it focuses on the worth of what a property can reasonably be used for compared to the land value and depreciated value of any improvements and any zoning restrictions -- in other words, if the best use of the land is to build condos or drill for oil.

ASK YOURSELF

1. Based on what this chapter covers, if you're an existing Airbnb owner, how does your property stack up, given the metrics we've covered? Does it still make sense for you to go ahead, given the goals you have in mind and the options available to you?
2. Is there anything you can do to improve the attractiveness of your property? This is an especially important consideration if you're currently renting out your primary residence as an Airbnb. Later in the book we'll look at ways of doing this.
3. If you're a potential Airbnb owner, after reading this chapter, what can you think of to improve your chances of succeeding in gaining the goals you have in mind for Airbnb? Do you have a property in mind?

I hope this chapter's been an encouragement. Really, what seem like huge problems can usually be overcome. Assuming you're still with us, then, in the next chapter you'll learn how to impress your guests through proper preparation of the Airbnb property in pursuit of those all-important positive guest reviews!

CHAPTER 2 - FURNISH TO IMPRESS

KEY TAKEAWAY:
The main point of this chapter is to first get an idea of the overall Airbnb demographics, then figure out what kind of guests will be your bread and butter, then how to decorate to attract them.

WE TRAVELED AROUND THE MEDITERRANEAN COASTLINE IN Turkey one summer near Olympos and stayed in a treehouse B&B. It was one of the more delightful places we encountered that year. I still remember it fondly.

Later in Cappadocia, Turkey, we stayed in a B&B dug out of a fairy chimney tower of soft volcanic ash. That was definitely the summer for interesting, offbeat accommodations!

So why would someone in their right mind build a B&B as a treehouse, furnished with a futon, cushions and quilts?

Demographics. The owners understood that the kind of people who go exploring around the Mediterranean coast in the summer are the kind of people who think a treehouse B&B is a great idea. They know who their customers are.

Put that same wonderfully funky treehouse in Las Vegas and no, nobody's staying there. The demographics are as wrong, as if you took one of those airport motels along I-490 to O'Hare Airport and plunked it down on the Mediterranean coast.

And try furnishing a business hotel's suite with only futons, cushions and quilts. You can imagine the reviews. The treehouse, however, gets glowing reviews.

The point is, of course, that you have to understand who your guest is and give them what they want. The treehouse owners understand their guests. Business hotels do. Cheap airport motels do too. You need to as well. This means getting a handle on who uses Airbnb the most, and this means studying demographics.

UNDERSTANDING AIRBNB DEMOGRAPHICS

As of 2017, the world statistics data for the age groups that used Airbnb were, according to Stratosjets:

- 36% between ages 25 and 34.
- 23% between ages 35 and 44.
- 15% between 18 and 24.
- 14% between 45 and 54.
- 7% between 55 and 64.
- 5% age 65 and older.

Yes, if you're running an Airbnb, you're mostly dealing with millennials, people between about 25 and 40 years old, and Gen Zers, those under 25. Those two demographic groups account for about 75% of all Airbnb guests -- in fact, millennials alone account for 60% of *all bookings ever* of the 500 million people who have used Airbnb since the very first one in 2008.

The number of senior citizens using Airbnb -- as both guests and hosts -- is growing, and this is a good thing. In certain places it's a smart move to cater to this group, but it's still a relatively small slice of the overall business. Basically, an Airbnb will attract people 40 and under.

There. That's your demographic sweet spot.

So you can see the importance of understanding your target guest before diving into hosting on Airbnb, as this determines key aspects in decorating to make your property as attractive as possible for potential guests. This in turn generates as many positive reviews as possible, and we've already gone over the inestimable importance of those.

Among millennials there are different types of guests -- the first timer who's never stayed in an Airbnb before, the foodies, families with young children, the young professional tired of corporate hotels, the explorer, not to mention the retirees and other guests. We'll discuss them in a bit more detail below.

But first, there are certain things you can do to put all guests in a good mood as soon as they walk in your property. These positive vibes are crucial for making that "Well! This is nice!" impression.

What you want to do, right off the bat, is appeal to your guests' five senses. Of course you want things to look their best, and make sure there aren't any dead rotting animal smells, okay, but don't forget that people have more than just sight (and smell). What your property sounds and feels like matters greatly.

Sight

This is, plenty of experts agree, the most important sense. Heaven help you if the property doesn't match up to the promotional photos on the site. That's a bad impression and it will be very difficult for the guest to shake. It almost doesn't matter what you do or how wonderful the place actually is after that, if they feel like they've been suckered with a bait and switch you are not getting a positive review, word of mouth or repeat business.

Of course it goes without saying that everything in the property is clean, in good repair, tidy and displayed to good advantage.

Smell

Fresh flowers? Yes! Smell is one of the most powerful triggers for emotion, either positive or negative. I've seen savvy real estate agents have aromatic coffee brewing and fresh-baked cinnamon rolls out in their open houses.

You can also use aromatherapy scents with a plug-in oil diffuser. Be sure you don't overdo it; you want it to be almost subliminal, like the guest feels good but doesn't really understand why, not like they just stumbled into a peppermint factory.

It's standard good practice to use dryer sheets for the linen to give it that fresh, clean scent. Put a dryer sheet in the linen closet so the extra linens smell good.

When it comes to smell please be mindful of your guests needs. It's always best to check with clients first to see if they have any allergies; many people prefer non-scented products. There was a couple who stayed with us who was highly allergic to scented dryer sheets, scented candles, plug-in air fresheners etc. To accommodate them, we removed all these things before they arrived and also cleaned the home 2 days before their arrival. They were so happy and have now become friends to our family. Since that first visit and have become annual visitors to our property in Barbados and stay for 4-6 weeks. It pays off to be accommodating to your guests and build relationships.

Taste

Have refreshments ready and visible when they walk in. Chilled bottled water and some cold and hot drink options are a must.

They've just finished traveling, and they're looking for a pick-me-up. Fresh fruit is a good option that appeals to everyone, not just for taste but for sight as well. Pay attention if the guest has indicated any dietary preferences, and put together a little welcome basket of appropriate snacks. Home-baked goodies are always appreciated!

The secret is that the guest doesn't have to actually eat the snack, or anything from the welcome basket. Their sense of taste will be stimulated with just the sight and smell of tasty food, and they'll appreciate the thoughtful gesture, especially if there are homemade items. Homemade says, "I care a little bit more and made that extra effort."

Sound

If it's possible given your setup to have SOFT -- I emphasize soft -- music playing when the guests arrive, do so. Light classical music is good, cocktail jazz for a bit more uptempo impression, or even some bossa nova if it fits the overall presentation of the property. Don't play elevator music; you can find inoffensive good quality music without resorting to that.

If the sounds outside are pleasant and calming, leave a window open if it's seasonally appropriate. This is a practice I regularly follow and highly recommend.

Touch

This one's a bit more subtle than the others, but having soft blankets on chairs or the sofa for the guest to curl up with is important. Imagine the difference between soft cotton and a more firm fabric suitable for a picnic blanket! Consider throw pillows, too. There's a surprising range of textures and firmness to them, so try them out yourself and go with what's most comfortable to you.

IMPRESSING THE DIFFERENT GUEST TYPES

Some good practices for STRs are common to all, such as the advice on appealing to all five senses above. But yes, there are things you can do to tailor the Airbnb experience to give guests that "Wow!" experience.

Spoiler alert: They all boil down to giving the guest the feeling that you went out of your way, did something you really didn't have to do, *just for them*. People *love* that feeling, and it's not as hard to do as you may think. Even if it's not exactly to their preference, just the simple fact that you tried, made an effort you didn't have to make to please them and to make their experience just that much better, goes a long, long way.

My wife and I were traveling through northern Italy years ago, in a remote area where Americans hadn't been seen much. The proprietor of the B&B I was staying at put an old copy of *Vogue* magazine, which I have absolutely no idea how he could have come by, in my room. Just because, you know, it was an American magazine, and I was American, and he thought I might like to have an American magazine to read.

Coincidentally my wife and I love fashion design and Vogue. It was so satisfying to curl up on the couch with a glass of wine and flip the pages of a vintage Vogue magazine. That gesture meant so much to us. He was thinking of what we might like, and going out of his way just to try his best to please me. It was personal, it was a surprise, it wasn't expecting any kind of reward, and it's still one of my sweetest travel memories.

So, let's take a look at some of the most common types of people you'll be dealing with and how to deal with them. You probably won't be all things to all people, but over time you'll come to recognize the primary three or four types of guests you get, and tailor your property to suit them (without scaring off the others, of course):

Event attendees. This traveler is in town for a specific reason, be it a concert, sports event, festival, wedding, and wants a cheap accommodation that has something interesting about it. In some ways, they're the easiest guests to please, since your STR isn't the focus of their stay. They're happy if things are clean, comfortable and as advertised.

- **How to deal:** Put all the travel and access information you can in a prime location. If you know what specific event they're attending, personalize travel info for that venue. If they'll be using public transport, type out the bus or train information on a smaller card they can take with them (we're going the extra mile, remember).
- **Protip:** Don't bother giving taxi information unless there is no Uber or Lyft service in your area. Millennials use rideshares if they don't have their own car or a prearranged ride. I can't remember the last time anybody's asked me for the number of the local taxi service.

First timers. They've stayed in hotels whenever traveling because that's just what they've always done. They've heard about "this Airbnb thing" long enough where they're willing to give it a try, especially after seeing the money they'll save. They've usually done a lot more research on your property than any other type of guest.

- **How to deal:** First timers need you to be as present as possible. Be there to greet them and kindly, gently answer all their "Now, I know this is a dumb question, but…" questions. They want to feel safe, reassured and confident that they're making the right decision, stepping out in the great unknown, the wild world of STRs.

Energetic retirees. This is a fast-growing market for Airbnb and it might make a lot of sense, depending on the area you're in, to cater to this demographic -- they have money and they want to spend it having a good time. These are people who usually had successful careers, and are probably experienced travelers. Now that they're retired they don't want to play shuffleboard, they want to continue traveling and seeing new things. They like kitchen luxuries, and knowing about interesting local destinations they probably haven't heard of. They're not disabled, but they like seeing that a property is easy to get around in.

- **How to deal:** Type out or make photocopies of all instructions for all the appliances, laminate them and put them all in a clearly-marked "INSTRUCTIONS FOR APPLIANCES" folder on the kitchen counter. Include the shower and the TV -- *especially* the TV. Seriously. This is one of the best Airbnb tips I ever got. I pass it along with my blessing.
- **For that really glowing positive review:** If they're up for it, brew some coffee and ask about their travel stories. Ninety-nine times out of a hundred I've found older, experienced travelers interesting, and they so enjoy telling someone new their stories. It makes a wonderful, wonderful impression.

Families with young children. These travelers want comfort, safety, reliability and dependability. They don't want to deal with the sort of interesting problems that were fun back when they were single and backpacking through Chile. They want to know what they're getting into and they want as much unpredictability removed from their stay as possible. They want a break from their normal routine, but not complete chaos. They're looking for STRs that emphasize "child friendly and safe."

- **How to deal:** Childproof the property as much as possible so parents don't have to sweep the house for potential hazards (they will anyway, of course). Show the parents where to put items they want to hide during their stay. Anything breakable that's of value, remove it. Put as many age-appropriate toys and furnishings in the property as possible, like high chairs, cribs, play pens, strollers -- any big items they'd rather not have to pack themselves.

Groups. This doesn't just mean stag weekends or bachelorette parties. These days, business brainstorming weekends, family reunions, encounter groups, and church retreats are more likely to take place in STRs that add interesting variety to their trip, not to mention that Airbnbs usually costs less than hotels do. They're looking for bigger properties with enough bedrooms, plenty of parking and ample kitchen facilities.

- **How to deal:** They don't need hand-holding; they usually have their time planned out. If you know the nature of the event, maybe you can leave a thoughtful welcome gift -- a bottle of Zinfandel for the bachelorettes, say.

Disabled travelers. Obviously, accessibility is the primary concern here. Disabled travelers check pictures and write-ups very carefully. If this is a market you'd like to cater to, make sure they know that clearly on the listing. Proactively encouraging disabled guests is hugely reassuring, as they know you'll have thought of the little things that matter to them.

- **How to deal:** Provide a picture gallery of the special disability access modifications you've made to the property. Let them know you don't mind if they rearrange the furniture, and assure them not to worry about putting everything back as they found it.

Cultural enthusiasts. Like the event traveler, this is a pretty easy guest to deal with. They're not there for your property; they just want a cheap place to crash while enjoying whatever cultural event they're there to soak up. This is not to say you can let things slide (you never do that), but just that you have to focus on getting the basics right and leave a culturally-appropriate gift on the counter.

- **How to deal:** If there is anything you can do to gussy up your property in line with the local culture, you might want to check it out.

Business travelers. These people are on business, yes, but they're sick of business hotels, and figure as long as they're in town they'll stay in a more interesting STR instead -- as long as it has sufficiently fast Internet and work spaces. They're looking for a roomy (ever notice how business hotels are somehow always cramped?), comfortable property close enough to their business destination and close to transport. If you impress them, they're highly likely to return and give you good word of mouth, as well as a solid gold review, but they're harder to impress than your casual vacationer. They expect everything to be *right*.

- **How to deal:** Give them what they want -- comprehensive business functionality with personalized charm. Make check-in and check-out as smooth and fast as possible. Show that you have the well-lit, roomy, fully wired work space they'll need, and a printer, an iron, a full-length mirror, and a Nespresso machine. Let them know you have extra chargers if they misplace or lose theirs. Don't forget they're still business travelers: Yes they're enjoying the STR experience, but they still want things to run as smoothly and predictably as at a five-star business hotel. The last thing they want to deal with are unexpected hassles and distractions. If you can offer personal shopping services while they're in town, weigh adding it to the bill against letting it be a pleasant surprise that will really boost your property in their mind and reviews. I've found that "I'm happy to pick up an order for you, no charge" gives that "Wow!" factor. And come on, how long does it actually take?

Foodies. These folks are in your area to sample the local cuisine. Attract them by emphasizing local food or wine festivals, or links to prominent restaurants (which might give you discount coupons for cross-promoting their eatery).

- **How to deal:** Feature pictures of your wonderful kitchen with a wide range of appliances, high-quality non-stick pans and quality knives. A welcome gift of local jam, jellies or cheeses would be a very thoughtful touch.

Lovebirds. They want a quiet, private, chill place to relax. If you have a spa or jacuzzi, feature that. They're probably celebrating some anniversary or other special day, and might appreciate ideas for interesting, offbeat local date activities. Otherwise, just put your best foot forward. But you were already doing that anyway, weren't you?

- **How to deal:** Basically, give them space and make yourself scarce. If there's anything particularly romantic about your property or your area make sure there are pictures. A nice bottle of Champagne or wine or box of chocolates on the counter is a tactful, much-appreciated touch.

Those are the basic categories of STR guests. Based on who you think your target guest and target demographic are, you can cater to their interests and taste. Not that you have to follow all these suggestions to a T; just pick what works for you and go with that.

Have good lighting. I put this first for a reason. It might be just me, but few things wreck a place more surely than bad lighting. Friends, this is a bigger consideration than you might realize! People can always have less light, but it is so, so maddening (to me anyway) not to be able to have enough light. In addition to adequate ceiling lighting, make sure, please, that there are enough reading lamps placed strategically in comfy reading nooks and by the sofa, and bedside lamps you can actually use to read while in bed. True story: I have gone out and bought more powerful light bulbs than the dingy ones at whatever property I'm staying at. Do not force your guests to resort to such desperate measures.

Consider your location. If you're just renting out your home in a heavily-traveled location, decor might not be as big a consideration. Obviously you're still going to be tasteful, but it isn't a selling point.

Follow a theme. If your STR is the destination, rather than just affordable accommodation near the destination, you'll have to put a lot more thought and effort into decor. What is there about your location that could work as an attractive theme for your property? Does a nautical theme work? Historical? Funky chic? Don't get cutesy, and don't overdo it unless you're catering to a *very specific* kind of guest ("Huh, I didn't know they made Dallas Cowboys toilet seats").

Spruce up the outdoor space. I confess: I do not have a green thumb. I would be the last person to ask about landscaping. I happily pay gardeners to work their magic. I give them a budget and say, "Do what works." It's worth every penny.

Make your interior design yours. Most guests don't want neutral, generic, one-size-fits-all decorating. They can get that at the chain hotel. Personal touches, whether they're specific to the guest's personal taste or not, impress a guest, especially if you use them in the following ways below.

- **Tell a story.** Once in Australia, I stayed in the home of a retired hydraulics engineer who had filled it with African art. Naturally, I asked about it, and heard some wonderful stories about her time in Africa. The

fact that it was a relatively conventional suburban home served to set the African decor off even more effectively. Even well-placed souvenirs or pictures of interestingly different locales can spark interest in a guest.
- **Find design inspiration.** If you salivate at the thought of scrolling through endless cute Pinterest and Instagram pictures, well, have at it. Personally, I've rarely trawled online sites for decor inspiration since I get ideas from my own travel, but I'm aware that you Pinterest pirates are out there. More power to you.
- **Green the place.** Plants and flowers are wonderful for giving a place a lively feel. There are plenty of low-maintenance plants that won't make your life difficult – just ask the folks down at the garden shop. They'll be happy to share their expertise, and suggest creative plant ideas you may not have considered -- as well as gently steering you away from any toxic or rash-causing plants.
- **Buy high-quality furniture.** Saving a few bucks by cutting corners with cheap furniture is another false economy. In the long run, it pays off to buy quality stuff that will last. Cheap is cheap, and guests can tell. Again, unless your chief selling point is your location and price, the impression your furnishings make is important.
- **Add bold accents.** Paint the front door green (assuming your neighborhood covenants allow it). Hey, it creates an impression. It stands out. Get a funky, somewhat inscrutable piece of art and let the guest wonder what it "means." Or go kitschy and hang a velvet Elvis. Why not?

- **Use small spaces.** Don't let space go to waste when you could do something interesting with it. Reading corners are nice.
- **Create comfortable workspaces.** This is especially true if you're catering to business travelers (see above), but any guests are going to be online. Give them a nice place to sit and surf.

ASK YOURSELF

1. Take your Airbnb space on a senses test drive. Does it meet the criteria for an impressive space based on the five senses?
2. Consider the guests you think will frequent your Airbnb -- your most common type of guest. Does the property cater to their needs? Would they see your listing and say "Yes! THAT is where I must stay!"?
3. Is there anything else you can do to improve your Airbnb property's appeal?

Great. Now let's see how to create the perfect pricing points.

CHAPTER 3 - P IS FOR PRICE

KEY TAKEAWAY:
The main point of this chapter is to help readers figure out the right price for their Airbnb.

THERE'S A CLASSIC CARTOON OF TWO BOYS AT A LEMONADE stand. Painted on the stand is "Lemonade -- $100 a glass." One of the boys is saying to the other "Look, all we need to do is sell one glass!"

This raises the issue of pricing: How do you determine what the best guest price is for your Airbnb property?

Airbnb is massively successful around the world. I've seen statistics indicating there are over 5.6 million listings over 220 countries.The main factor driving all that success, of course, is price. Airbnb saw that hotels were getting a little overpriced for what they delivered, and jumped in.

They found that people agreed -- some estimates are that hotels lose about $450 million *per year* to STRs. So you can see why they're fighting against us so tenaciously, and why their lobbyists are pushing so hard for anti-STR zoning and other restrictive local governmental regulations.

But millions and millions of travelers like what we offer, and as wonderful and attractive as your property is on its own merits, pricing is the straw that stirs the drink. So we need to figure out how to price your property so that it's low enough to attract bookings, but high enough to leave you with enough profit at the end of the day to make it all worthwhile.

It's difficult, sure. If it were easy, everyone would be doing it. Finding the optimal price for your property in your area involves a lot of work. But it's worth it, since pricing is the make or break factor in your whole Airbnb adventure. Get it right and you win, but get it wrong, and well...

First, however, you need to decide what your overall pricing strategy is.

This is more important than you may have realized. Pricing isn't a question of what price tag you are going to slap on a product. It's determining what's the best long-term way of growing your business. Every business has to decide if its strategy is margin or volume -- if it wants to sell a lot of things with a small profit margin on each, or fewer things but with a higher profit margin for each sale.

In other words, you have to decide if you want high occupancy rates but low profit per occupancy, or low occupancy rates with a higher profit on each one. I know, you want high occupancy with a high profit on each. We all do. But we each have to decide which side of the balance we're going to lean to -- volume or margin.

And please, remember that there is no single perfect price for all year round. Your rates will adjust as the market does. Pricing is not set-and-forget unless you have a really unique property and strategy.

So here are some common STR pricing strategies for you to consider:

THE MAXIMUM FILL RATE APPROACH

This is also known as the "get as many warm bodies in your property as possible" mentality. It's relatively easy to accomplish: just throw out a really low nightly price. You'll get bookings, and you'll have a dependable cash flow.

But will you be making a profit? Will you be making enough profit to make it worth your time? High turnover means a lot more work and near-constant attention to the business. If that's your thing, if you want to focus on the STR all day, then great. This'll work for you.

Now bear in mind that this could work as a short-term fill instead of a default strategy. You don't keep your price the same all year round, and there might be times in the year when it makes sense to drop your nightly rate from an average of, say, $85 a night to $20 a night. Sure you're taking a (much) lower profit per guest, but you're at least getting cash in the door. You're staying afloat for when the good times come back around again.

In general, maximum fill rate works well if you're an individual host or a fully-fledged vacation rental management company who can afford to do this full time. For people who (like me) want Airbnb to supplement their income, and not consume all their bandwidth, it's not. I have friends who swear by max fill rate. It works for them, and that's great. For them.

I've used maximum fill rate from time to time to tide me over rough patches, but it's not my daily go-to pricing strategy. I have a life outside of Airbnb.

THE MAXIMUM RATE PER NIGHT APPROACH

This is selling lemonade at $100 a glass: great work if you can get it, and you don't need too many sales.

With this strategy you get fewer bookings, but you pocket more profit on each one. You spend less time working the property, and you have fewer hassles and issues to deal with. You're still making a profit, but you're not spending all your waking hours and attention on Airbnb. You're living your life and getting some money on the side.

You can see who would favor this approach. It works well for a really unique property that stands out, that would almost qualify as a destination property in its own right. It's a good strategy if you own a premium property, since Airbnb does attract people who are looking for that kind of thing, be it a house in the middle of a private island, a penthouse with a great view of the skyline, a place on the top of a mountain, a house built during the American Revolution, somewhere Bob Dylan once lived, a house reputed to be haunted or whatever the prime selling point is.

This strategy works great for attracting wealthy travelers looking to stay in premium places. The drawback, of course, is that there simply aren't all that many wealthy travelers who are not price-conscious out there, and there's stiff competition for them. But if you have a really wonderfully unique property, and you're happy just having it occupied now and then, max rate per night would be a good approach for you.

THE LONG-TERM APPROACH

This is going after the longer stay market, where you rent out the STR property by the week or by the month.

This is great if you're in a more tightly-regulated STR market, or a high-demand area. For example, I live in a town which is considered a regional vacation destination, and my neighbor simply goes away for the summer and over long school vacations and accepts one rental to cover the time she's away. That works for her – she's not into nightly guests even though she could make more money managing it per night, since short stay nightly rates are by definition higher than longer term rentals when averaged out to nightly rates.

What's good about this strategy is that there's a lot less time and effort required on your part. You also avoid losing money on unoccupied nights. Adrian, who we met at the beginning of this book, does this, and in North London it works. It doesn't work in all areas.

It also can involve things like signing rental agreements, showing the property before someone commits, listing the property on other platforms, and usually lowering nightly prices to attract a longer term commitment, so you're sacrificing per night profit.

But it can work if you have to be away for a couple weeks or a month at a time and you want your house generating some sort of return during that time. If you're a full-time property manager, this can be a good option.

THE COMBINATION APPROACH

As the name implies, this method uses all the aforementioned pricing strategies whenever each one makes the most sense. This is the best way to maximize profits from running an STR, since it allows you to do whatever boosts your occupancy and finds the best prices.

This is the strategy to adopt if you really want to focus on Airbnb as your primary income (or if you have a property management team), because let me tell you, it's profitable, sure, but it's a lot of work, a lot of time and a lot of hassle. I tried this for a couple years, but went back to more of a blend of the long term and maximum rate per night approaches. I found I just wasn't that driven by profit to make it worth my time, but if you are, this is the way to do Airbnb right.

What you do with the combination approach is get long-term deals during the slow season, and go to max per night or max fill in during the high season. Again, this is lucrative but it's also a real job. Pursue this strategy if you simply want to make as much money as you can from your property and you have the time and energy to concentrate on it.

So you've determined which overall, big picture pricing strategy works for you. Again, you can switch between them as needed, as seasons and other considerations dictate, but you need to settle on one as your primary approach.

Now. That done, how do you go about determining what to actually charge guests?

First, understand that there are five primary pieces of the pricing puzzle for Airbnb:

1. The nightly rate. This is defined as the price per night per guest. It's higher for short stays (one or two nights) and lower for fixed long-term stays. Calculate your nightly cost as a guide to setting the nightly rate. Add up all monthly expenses, taxes, mortgage, Value-Added Tax (VAT) if that applies in your area, and divide by 30. That's your nightly cost. Your nightly rate needs to cover that over a year. Look at what similar properties in your area are charging.

2. The cleaning fee. You can, if you want, tack on a cleaning fee to the nightly rate. Some Airbnb owners do this. I don't. People assume the property will be clean when they get there and that you'll clean it after they leave, and that this expense is baked into the nightly rate. When it comes to pricing, as with the rest of my overall Airbnb strategy, I favor simplicity, mainly because guests trust and appreciate it more, and simplicity means giving one price for a stay. I factor the cleaning cost into the nightly rate and just quote that one price. When determining if you should charge a cleaning fee, be sure to research your competition. If other Airbnbs in your area are charging a cleaning fee, you should be able to as well. Research will also help determine the acceptable rate.

3. Any other charges. Please, don't do this except for things that are *genuinely* extra expensive for you to offer. I've seen Airbnbs add a "Wi-fi fee," a "parking fee," and other nonsense. This is just wrong. This looks like nickel and diming guests. Extra charges are for things like preparing meals, or putting together picnic baskets; they're not for leaving a couple bicycles at the property or bathroom amenities.

- Now, charging for an extra guest is a bit more fluid. Does the extra guest really add work and expense for you? If so, it's fine to charge extra. Most people expect to pay extra for an extra guest, so even if they don't increase your operating expense you can still charge. There's nothing wrong with you making a profit, after all, just don't be so... chintzy about adding extra charges for using the TV and the like -- "There's a $2 charge for each DVD you play." Don't laugh. People have done it.

4. Security deposit. I do collect a fully refundable security deposit and I am *very* hesitant to dip into it unless there's significant damage -- remember that New Year's Eve party I mentioned? Yeah, they never saw their security deposit again. Guests expect a security deposit. It's not considered offensive if you ask for a reasonable sum to cover damage, especially if it's your home you're renting out as an STR. But it's not a source of extra income for you. The security deposit is for major expenses, not normal wear and tear. It's for repairing broken furniture or replacing a missing lamp, not for scrubbing a little crayon off the wall.

5. Discounts. At your discretion. Especially if you're just starting out, listing a new property, it's wise to offer a discounted price to get those good reviews and word of mouth going. Occasional seasonal promotions -- Valentine's Day Getaway Special For Two! -- are good ideas.

Those are the basic pricing factors. Now let's see what else you need to consider:

Location.

This is a biggie, probably *the* biggie. Your location determines demand to a large extent, and higher-demand areas can get away with charging more for accommodation than rarely-traveled places. Some Airbnbs serve areas with a pretty steady demand, and they can keep their prices high year-round. If this is your situation, the gods have smiled on you. Baraka.

For most Airbnbs, the demand is cyclical. It could be seasonal. If you run an STR in Vermont, you're most busy from about late September through October and your prices are the highest they are all year. For the rest of the year, not so much, and your prices go down.

Or, the cycles could be event-based. If you're in Indianapolis you can charge more when the Indy 500 is on than when it's not, or in Louisville for the Kentucky Derby, etc.

If there are big festivals or other regularly-scheduled events in your area, generally speaking prices go up because accommodation is more scarce, and in Economics 101 they teach you that scarcity and demand drive pricing.

The property itself.

How desirable is your STR? What amenities do you offer? Are you on a lake with a dock and you offer kayaks and fishing tackle? You can charge more than can a virtually identical property six miles from anything.

Is yours a nice, big, sprawling property on a large tract of land with beautiful vistas? Is it on the coast with great views of the ocean? Is it overlooking the city which is beautiful at night? That's money in the bank for you. More affluent travelers will pay more to be in that setting than a smaller house in a suburb.

Do you have a hot tub? Price goes up. Are you offering a shared space? Price goes down. In the middle of all the action? Price goes up. Noisy but not really close to much? Down.

Who's your target guest?

All through this book so far, we've spent quite a bit of time discussing which guests would be most attracted to your STR. By now, you should have a fair idea of who's going to be your usual guest.

If it's the more affluent traveler, you can get away with charging more because you have something that appeals to them. If yours is more of an Airbnb catering to students and backpackers, well, you charge less, but you have higher occupancy.

Families and groups are willing to pay more, as are business travelers. Price-conscious event and cultural travelers are more interested in finding a good deal.

Understand your expenses.

See above. You should be able to come pretty close in figuring how much each guest costs you, and how much your property is costing you. Now you need to set a price, depending on your pricing strategy above, that leaves you with enough profit to help you reach your Airbnb goal, whether that's a full-time supporting income or a side hustle.

No matter what your pricing strategy is, it has to work out to profit by the end of the year, not week by week or even month by month. In other words, it's okay to lose money during the slow season if you make it back and more once things start heating up, if by the end of the year you can show net profit.

Don't forget to think about capital expenses, too. How often do you have to get the place repainted to keep it attractive? How long will the major appliances last? Does the electricity need rewiring? How's the roof?

Study the competition.

Do market research. When I started out, I stayed in a few Airbnbs in my area to get a good feel for what they provide, what travelers expect, what I thought made a property overpriced and what seemed to me to be a good deal.

Be constantly scrutinizing all the listings in your area. I mean, three or four times a week. What do you notice changing? Looking at the listings, is your property positioned where you want it, either towards the "good price" end or the "great property" end of things? Are properties as nice as yours charging noticeably more or less than you are, or more or less than they were charging last month?

What's their cancellation policy? What amenities do they offer? How do their reviews look? How does all of that compare with your property and price?

Just to offer a lesson from my experience: I have a cool property, so I thought I'd get a jump starting out by listing it for a really low price. Generally, that's a sound strategy; starting out you should offer lower prices to get traction. I got bookings and great reviews, which helped in the long run, but the strategy backfired in the short run and I ended up losing serious money because I didn't realize that many destination-oriented travelers *want to pay higher prices* for better properties. I hadn't researched my competition well enough to know what I could have been charging for what I was offering to the traveler I was hoping to attract.

The reasoning is that people naturally assume if a property's really good, it'll be more expensive, and if it's not pricey there's something wrong with it. I guess it's the same principle I use when buying wine. Knowing nothing about wine myself, I tend to correlate quality with price, figuring a $45 bottle of Merlot will be a better wine than its $15 a bottle cousin.

But this is the art of pricing -- you lose money both by overpricing and underpricing.

Your price has to match your goals.

As we've been saying, do you want this to be a full-time gig or an extra revenue stream for minimal effort? How much money do you need to be making for that to happen?

Analytics-based pricing tools.

The good news is there are plenty of analytics-based pricing tools to help you corral all the various pricing factors. AirDNA (www.airdna.co), AllTheRooms (www.alltherooms.com), and Transparent (www.seetransparent.com) are three I've used and can recommend. There are others. Some people swear by Wheelhouse (www.usewheelhouse.com). I haven't used it much myself, but I hear good things about it from people I trust.

Know the platform itself inside and out.

You really have to be an expert on Airbnb itself, and the STR industry in general. You have to know all the options the platform offers, how you can take advantage of it and make it work for you and what are the reasonable expectations you can have.

Know how to set the nightly rate (Go to "Your listings," pick the one you want to price, click "Pricing" on that page, find "Nightly price" and click "Edit," pick your price and "Save." Voilà.). Know that, in fact, Airbnb offers helpful tools to aid you in deciding what price to set, and will suggest pricing options for you. Know how to use the Airbnb Smart Pricing (www.airbnb.com) tool.

(Hint: Some people find Airbnb's pricing tool to recommend a price lower than what they think it should be. Bear in mind that Airbnb makes their money from service fees based on how many bookings you get, not how much profit you make, so they're going to nudge you towards prices that increase bookings, which are not necessarily the prices that jibe with your own business goals. Just throwing that out there. Do with it what you will.)

Did you know that Airbnb allows you to set custom pricing for certain dates automatically, so you don't have to manually do it each time? Do you know all the automation tools the platform offers? Are you sure?

Know Airbnb's service fee structure so you don't get nasty surprises.

ASK YOURSELF

1. Based on everything we've covered in this chapter, and your own intuition and experience, figure out which pricing strategy would work best for your Airbnb property. Really, I can't overemphasize the importance of thinking in terms of the whole year. I've seen properties fail because the owner thought they had to show profit every week, so either wildly over- or underpriced their STR.
2. If you already have an Airbnb, do you feel like your pricing strategy works for you, and why? What can you do to improve the occupancy rate by optimizing the price?
3. Do you even want to increase your occupancy rate, or just the profit margin per occupancy?

Isn't pricing fun? The next chapter dives into the key points of creating a stellar listing.

CHAPTER 4 - THE TRIPLE FACTOR

KEY TAKEAWAY:
The main point of this chapter is to guide you in creating the perfect listing for your properties.

When it comes to listing your property, there's a trio of factors to getting the best results: Most every successful listing consists of great photos, a catchy title and an awesome -- and accurate! -- description. That's what we'll discuss how to accomplish in this chapter.

THE PICTURES

We'll start with the photos, since that's the part most people spend the most time on, if they aren't paying professional photographers to do it for them. In fact, some experts say that even if your descriptions and listing title are rather ordinary, if you have great pictures done right, that'll make up for it.

Myself, I work with a combination of mostly professionally-taken pictures with a few of my own shots of the little personal touches I want to emphasize. I try to put as much effort into my descriptions and title as I do the photos, but if writing isn't your strong suit and photography is, take heart -- a picture is worth a thousand words!

So here are seven general areas to work through to get really, really good photos for your Airbnb property.

1. Pre-photo work.

Get the place looking good, decluttered, arranged attractively, cleaned, etc. It's really hard to have attractive, appealing photos when the place isn't looking its best. Now, one mistake a lot of Airbnb newbies make is to try to cram all the attractive things they can think of in the pictures. No -- the secret I keep telling myself is KISS: Keep It Simple, Sweetheart!

- What you want to convey is a simple, basic idea of what your property has to offer. Clutter is not appealing. Clutter does not welcome people into your property. Clutter makes rooms look smaller and less comfortable than they actually are. It looks like you don't really care. Channel your inner Marie Kondo (celebrity organizing guru) and simplify, simplify, simplify.

2. The four areas you have to get right.

There are four rooms every potential guest looks at, whether they realize they're doing it or not, which form their general impression of your property. For other rooms, just follow the no-clutter rule and you'll be fine. Set the dining table as if you're having guests over. Put a bottle of wine and a couple glasses out on a balcony table. The principle here is for guests to look at the picture and imagine themselves in it, enjoying themselves:

- **The kitchen.** It is highly important to get this right. Bowls of fresh fruit make any kitchen look better. Clean cabinets in good repair are great. If you have open shelves, make sure the plates, cups, glasses, etc. are neat and organized. Show the coffee maker that the guest will actually get to use. Again, remember that simplicity, not clutter, is the look you want -- don't think that putting all the fancy appliances and gizmos in one shot will impress guests. Put out one or two of the best ones, preferably one. I splurged for a really cool retro toaster, and since it's the only counter appliance in my pictures, I make sure people see it.
- **The bedroom.** White sheets and linens, please. If you have well-done, tasteful quilts, put these on the bed. No yucky brown or gold duvets unless they're an integral part of the decorating theme, and make sure there are splashy colors somewhere else in the room. Art prints always make a bedroom look better, especially if they match the overall color scheme you

have going on. A tastefully-positioned mirror is a nice, subtle addition to a brightly-colored bedroom.
- **The bathroom.** I don't have to tell you to make doubly sure everything is as clean, tidy, and in as good condition as possible here. Again, please, KISS -- bath towels for each guest, hand towels, toilet paper, hand soap, hair dryer and garbage can. Ensure towels and details are color-coordinated.
- **The living room (lounge).** Probably the hardest room to declutter, but do your best. No coasters on table tops unless they add color to an otherwise dull look. Colorful rugs work well and throw rugs break up large spaces, and books on coffee tables are really good. Fold some blankets and put some throw pillows around to imply relaxation and comfort, making sure the colors enhance (rather than clash with) the feel of the room.

3. There are some technical photographic practices that help you get better pictures.

In general, this is why I let pros do this for me, as they have filters and settings and lenses I don't, and nine times out of ten they can get really good shots I can't. But if you're using your own equipment, make sure you put the HDR (High Dynamic Range) setting on, since it evens out the light exposure so light coming in a window doesn't make the rest of the room look dark or smaller.

- Professional photographers tell me that morning and late afternoon are the best times for natural light (general rule: Natural light is the best light). They try to shoot with the sun behind the photo, and they always take horizontal rotations (that's the "landscape" setting), never vertical, when featuring a real estate property, since it makes the rooms look bigger. This is especially important if you're trying to use your phone camera to take pictures, which I do not recommend -- if you're going to take pictures yourself and you're not a trained or experienced photographer, at least use a good quality camera and tripod. The difference is noticeable.

- Size matters: Airbnb recommends a photo size of 1024 x 683px. Use a width to length aspect ratio of 3:2. Follow their recommendations, and resize your photos if you have to.
- Another nifty trick is to point your camera to the corner of a room when taking pictures. It's a more interesting perspective, it makes the whole room look bigger and more inviting. Stand as far back as possible when taking the picture. Experiment with angles, choosing the ones that show off the room to its best advantage.
- Don't shoot from eye level. Pros shoot from lower than eye level. Try waist level, making sure you keep the camera straight, not tilted.

4. Find something unique about your property to feature in the pictures.

When I said to avoid clutter, I didn't mean strip all objects from the rooms, I meant take out the ones that don't belong, the ones that present a confused look. Maybe one room can be a dedicated art room, or music room, or man cave, or a room obviously dedicated to professional work space. Each room should look welcoming and inviting. Open laptops and cups of coffee on a table are great touches. You want your guest to feel like they would enjoy being in that room.

5. Take great care presenting the kitchen.

Studies of STRs consistently find that guests are very interested in the quality of the kitchen. And this does not mean they want a huge commercial-grade kitchen with a thousand appliances; it means they want clean, functional kitchens, no matter the size, shown to their best advantage. If yours is a smaller kitchen without overhead racks of copper cookware, make sure the appliances shown are of good quality and sparkling clean. One or two attractive wall tiles or small pictures provide an inviting look. Remember, it's not "small," it's "cozy" and "homey," so make it appear so!

- Especially if you're selling a homey, cozy kitchen, put out a plate of homemade cookies, or a small charcuterie board with a glass of white wine on the counter. Remember, you want people thinking, "Wow, this is stunning. I want to be in *that* kitchen."

6. Do show some scenes of your property's surroundings.

If you're in a city, show some attractive features close to the property -- a cool restaurant, coffee shop or neighborhood pub. If you're on the water, that's a great location, so be sure to emphasize that. Any impressive views from your property? Make doubly sure potential guests can see them all. If you're in a more urban or suburban setting you can use Google Maps to show inviting local features like parks, running trails, historical points of interest or other attractive features. You can even post a screenshot of the Google or Apple Maps summary of your neighborhood.

7. Airbnb lets you post a hundred pictures, but you don't need that many to allow the guest to visualize every important aspect of their stay at your property.

Remember the no-clutter rule! I mean, really, have you ever scrolled through a hundred pictures to try to decide where to stay? I sure haven't. You'll be fine with a minimum of twenty and a maximum of thirty pictures.

- Arrange the photos as if you're actually giving a tour. Start with either the lounge or master bedroom and move through the four primary areas listed above, then one picture apiece of the other rooms, avoiding similar-looking photos (nobody needs six different angles of the shower). Then go outside for the views, surroundings, landscaping, etc.
- Caption each photo, not just "Kitchen" or "Patio." They can see it's a bedroom. Try "Enjoy stretching out and relaxing with a good book or a good friend on these comfortable sofas," or "This cozy little kitchen has everything you need to whip up some tasty meals." Remember, you're always trying to get the guest to think, "That is a place I'd like to be."
- Include significant outdoor areas like patios, pools, gardens and roof terraces, anything that would add to the guests being able to picture themselves enjoying the property -- a hammock if you have one, and if you can string a hammock, do so. Guests never use them as much as they think they will but they're a powerfully subtle way of saying, "You'll enjoy relaxing here."
- Make sure you have at least one clear, wide shot of

the entrance to your property so the guest will recognize it when they get there!
- Some experts say the first six or seven photos are the key ones, so to put the best one from each of the primary areas up top. Or if there's a really spectacular selling point about the view or surroundings, use that. The first photo of a room should be a corner shot.
- The purpose of the first photo overall is to get guests to continue clicking. Put your very best shot first. You'll really benefit from asking for friends' opinions on which one to feature. This is another advantage of hiring professional help with the pictures: they'll know which one to lead with, and that could make all the difference.
- Be creative. Airbnb hosts have been known to include a floor plan with the pictures, or photos of themselves and past guests (obviously with guests' permission), screenshots of directions to their place if it's particularly tricky, or even composite, collage-style pictures. I've seen listings with a screenshot of the Wi-fi speed test.

And one last piece of advice -- don't hide obvious flaws that the guest will see anyway. I mean, don't feature them, but let them show up in the corner of a picture. It's Airbnb, not a five-star hotel, and people get that. As long as it's not something that will impact their ability to be safe and comfortable in the property, be real. It boosts trust if guests know you're not just giving them the carefully airbrushed version.

THE TITLE

The title is not the biggest part of your Airbnb listing, but it's of key importance. It needs to be catchy without turning guests off by being over the top ("The BEST property in Oslo!"); it needs to pique interest while being clear.

So how to use the title to present the property to its best advantage and attract the most interest?

Glad you asked! iGMS has some formulas that work well, so let's take a look.

1. First, understand who it is you're pitching your property to. Who's your typical guest? Why are they staying at your property? "GREAT PARTY NIGHTLIFE VIBES!" does not pull in the retiree set. "Privacy for that romantic getaway" attracts couples. And never use all capital letters. Please.
2. Feature your property's #1 selling point. Free parking? Swimming pool? Ultra-fast Wi-fi? What sets you apart? Recent upgrades are always good if you're stuck.
3. Use abbreviations. There's a 50-character limit. You'll want to use all that and pack as much in as you can. Write w/ instead of "with." Boom, two characters saved. Use BR, BA, APT, AC, CBD, DT for bedroom, bathroom, apartment, air conditioned, central business district, downtown, etc.
4. Use emojis judiciously. A heart emoji with DT says "in the heart of downtown" with only three of your fifty precious characters. Use emojis sparingly. You don't want your title to be a puzzle or look like a junior highschool kid's text.

5. Use specific words instead of dull general words like "nice" or "good." Spice up the listing with "Insta-worthy," "Rare," "Renovated," "Peaceful," "Secluded," "Contemporary," "Resort," "Eclectic" and "Couple's Getaway."

Some good formulas are:

1. Adjective + Property Type w/ Top Features.

- "Cozy Private Cottage w/ Large Sauna + Mountain View." This attracts guests looking for a specific kind of property. "Rustic private cottage" gives a good idea of the location and vibe of the property. Guests can imagine themselves in just such a place looking out at the ocean; you almost don't need photos. And mentioning the king-size bed puts another attractive idea in the guests' minds -- everybody wants to know they'll get a good, comfortable night's sleep.

2. Adjective + Property Type + Near Landmark - Distance.

"Spacious 4BR Near Eiffel Tower -- 7 Min Walk." This title gives all the most important information quickly. Travelers will know immediately if it fits their most important considerations, and shows them how convenient the property is.

3. Adjective + Property Type + Perfect for + Experience.

- "Luxury Beach House Perfect for Romantic Weekend Getaway." Again, this is for a pretty specific kind of guest, and it grabs their attention. This is pretty close to the title I use for my Airbnb. It does a lot of the work for me in terms of funneling guests who are more likely to book my property and weeding out lots of repetitive inquiries that usually result in a "thanks, but no thanks" at the end. Basically using this approach tells the guest: "We understand you, we know what you're looking for and we have it."

4. Enjoy + Selling Point + at Adjective Property Type + in/at Location.

- "Enjoy Sunsets at Fully Equipped 2BR Condo at the Beach." This is a quite specific title. I originally used one much like it until I realized I was unnecessarily putting off guests who would have been pleased with the property, but who weren't looking for quite as narrow an experience. But for those who just want to watch sunsets over the beach from a two bedroom condo, this is solid gold.

5. Property Type + Selling Point + Selling Point.

- "Family Home w/ Free Parking & No-Hassle Check In." This is for the more pragmatically-inclined travelers who know what they want, are interested in getting the skinny quickly and will decide whether to keep clicking or not based on how their most important considerations are met.

Don't include borderline irrelevant information. It usually doesn't matter to say how many bedrooms there are in the title if you can use that space more effectively. They can see that in the writeup. Likewise, you probably don't need to get real specific about what neighborhood your property is in. Either the guest won't care or they're already searching in your area for a reason.

THE DESCRIPTION

With a catchy title and great pictures, your work is nearly done. The description is for pushing the wavering over the edge and into your property.

Rule #1: Be brief and concise. You don't need to explain everything, so please don't try. If your pictures clearly show it, you don't need the description to dwell on it.

Again, as with so much of succeeding in Airbnb, you simply must know who your target guest is. Think what words would appeal to them. "Comfortable," "convenient," "easy," and "simple" appeal to the older traveler. "Hip," "active," "kinetic," and "unpredictable" appeal to younger travelers. "Safe" appeals to families, and "cheap" appeals to a lot of people!

So, the parts of a good description:

1. The introduction. Your whole writeup is going to be brief and to the point, especially the introduction. It's your selling points listed in a couple sentences. After reading your title, seeing your pictures and reading your description's introduction, 95% of the guest's decision is made.

2. Room descriptions. My experience chatting with guests indicates that if they read past the introduction, they had already at least mentally decided they would like to stay at my property. They were just looking to see if any red flags jumped out. Or, I was so close with another property that they were trying to decide by vacuuming up all the information they could. But most often, the guest had decided by this point that I was one of the top contenders, or that I had the booking as long as nothing bad turned up in the rest of the description, like "large sewage spill nearby." So yes, describe the rooms, but in short paragraphs, writing as to someone who you know really likes the property already.

- Of course, it doesn't hurt to talk your place up a bit, after all. If you have lovely hardwood flooring that isn't obvious in the pictures, mention that. It tells the guest about more than the flooring; it paints a picture of a kind of place that has hardwood flooring, a place where other things are likely to be solid and classic as well.

3. Outdoors. Mention this only if there's something of note. Don't rattle on about how lovely the flowers are unless it's a major selling point of the property. Describe what there is that would help a guest visualize staying there -- are there toys or swings for kids? A pool? A croquet lawn?

4. Location. The guest already has a pretty good idea of the location from your title and pictures. Here's where you tell them if there's anything of note nearby, or if there's anything they should know about public transport, neighbors, restaurants or walking opportunities before deciding.

Now here are the three most important words for writing description:

Show, don't tell.

Don't *tell* the readers, "This is a relaxing property." *Show* them that "this property is ten miles from civilization." They get the point: It's quiet.

A certain amount of puffery is expected -- "You'll love the sweeping panoramic views of the harbor from the balcony, enjoying a glass of wine in the cool breeze." There's something to adding an element of desire to a description. I do it in my listings.

But I convey information, and you need to as well. In that sentence, the reader learns that the property has a balcony with nice views of the harbor. You're creating a mood while conveying information, which is fine, and the guest feels like they're in the property, which is great.

What you want to avoid is vague telling: "This is a comfortable property with many amenities to make sure your stay is relaxing and refreshing for you to recharge your batteries." What do you actually learn about the property?

Instead, write, "The property backs out onto a national park so evenings are quiet, and all you hear is the gentle lapping of the lake a few yards from the back door." That conveys the same feeling the first sentence does, but the guest learns facts.

Use words that match the tone you're setting. Are you offering convenience? Use words like "fast," "efficient," "convenient," "close" and "quick." Are you offering relaxation? Use "calm," "slow-paced," "secluded," "gentle" and "relaxing." Romance? Use "spicy," "exciting," "intimate," "lovely" or "romantic." You get the idea.

Read a dozen descriptions of properties on Airbnb, the top listings. You'll catch on to what they're doing. I hesitate to give too much direction, since the descriptions, ultimately, need to sound like you.

ASK YOURSELF

1. Can I really take pictures that would make my property look as good as a professional photographer could?
2. Is every character in my title pulling its weight?
3. Does my description show my property, or just say things?

You've gotten the guest in your property. The next chapter talks about how to be a successful host for that guest.

CHAPTER 5 - SUCCESSFUL HOSTING

KEY TAKEAWAY:
This chapter covers key aspects of successful hosting and how to become a better Airbnb host.

There are metrics you can use to determine whether you're a successful Airbnb host or not. Of course, there's the absolute bottom line of your bank account, and my favorite is the notes and reviews guests leave for me thanking me for a wonderful stay, but there are plenty of other ways to measure how you're doing objectively.

They include things like a great response rate, those all-important five-star reviews and positive marketing responses.

If you've read this far in this book, that means you want to improve your Airbnb hosting. If you're just starting out, you want to know the good habits to develop early in your Airbnb career. And if you're wondering how to go from being an adequate to a great host who gets more five-star reviews, somebody your guests remember, and eventually a member of the elite club of Superhosts, this chapter will help you achieve that.

It must be said that there is a hospitality gene. Some people, not as many as you'd think, just have a certain intuitive way with guests. You could put them in charge of hosting the worst property imaginable and they'd find ways of making the guests feel welcomed and special.

And of course there's the other extreme -- put these people in charge of hosting the nicest property imaginable and guests can still come away feeling slighted or ignored and have an overall negative guest experience.

You're somewhere in the middle, tending to one side or the other. If you're already a pretty good host, you can always improve, and if you're naturally a not-so-great host, you can learn to be welcoming in a way that feels sincere. Everyone has room to increase ratings, response rate and profits.

YOUR RESPONSE RATE

Airbnb calculates what's called a response rate. While Airbnb doesn't reveal everything that goes into determining each property's ranking on the platform, response rate is a very important factor in your property's success. And even though we don't know for sure all that goes into Airbnb's ranking formula, we do know there are things we can do to help improve it. Your response rate is a big part of that.

Response time. This measures the average amount of time you take to answer new guest inquiries and requests for bookings. Forget for now the fact that Airbnb allows for a 24-hour window for you to respond to a new guest inquiry or booking request (if you don't respond within 48 hours they'll put your listing on hold). You should be answering them as soon as you see them.

The good hosts, the ones your property is competing against for prime platform location, are answering their inquiries within a couple hours, not seeing how close to 24 hours they can get.

Not that you need to have all the answers they may be seeking in their initial inquiry; Airbnb just determines your response from your first email back to a potential guest. They don't pay attention to anything after that. So it's of the utmost importance that you get back to them ASAP to let them know they've been heard, you're glad they reached out to you and you're getting the specifics they need as fast as you can. A guest is usually inquiring at more than one property, so whoever gets back to them first has a huge advantage in securing the booking.

If you always respond within 24 hours in a 30-day period, your official response rate should be 100%. If you're a newer property with not as many inquiries, Airbnb will look at the past three months to calculate your response rate. Those with Superhost status have a 90%-plus response rate over the past year, but in reality if you're waiting 22 hours to respond you're losing business.

Acceptance rate. Your acceptance rate is how often you accept or decline reservations. This is different to your response rate because Airbnb does not count all guest inquiries to determine your acceptance rate. It's slightly confusing, so let me explain:

An **inquiry** is any email that comes in. "Can I bring my chihuahua?" "How close are you to the stadium?" "¿Habla español?" In other words, inquiries are not necessarily reservation requests. If you decline the inquiry, you're telling the person that your property is not a fit for them, and they should look elsewhere. Doing so does not impact your acceptance rate.

A **reservation request** is somebody formally asking to book your property. You must either approve or decline this within 24 hours. If you don't, it's automatically considered a decline. The higher the acceptance rate the more likely you are to be classified as an Airbnb Plus host and the better for where your listing gets ranked, although Airbnb does not disclose the exact formula they use.

Your acceptance rate does not affect your Superhost status, since they get more reservation requests than they can possibly accommodate.

Airbnb is very keen that its users should have a good experience, and response rate is part of the user experience -- imagine if you sent off a bunch of inquiries and nobody got back to you for days. You wouldn't want to use the platform again. Response rate isn't an arbitrary standard; it's actually a key metric for the success of Airbnb overall. So naturally, they're going to give better treatment to hosts who make inquiries part of a good user experience.

Using Airbnb's Instant Book feature is another good way to boost your rankings, but only if it makes sense for your property.

And if you were wondering if it really makes all that much difference to achieve Superhost status, it does: Superhosts make about 60% more daily revenue than other hosts. So it's worth it to pay close attention to your response rate, besides the fact that you're letting business slip through your fingers if you are not paying attention to the details.

Message templates are a godsend. I use them because they save lots and lots of time. I have one for just about any inquiry I can expect to get for every step of the process. They're not difficult -- take a look at your past inquiries. Most of them ask pretty much the same thing, am I right? Yes we have off-street parking. Sorry, but 2 p.m. is the latest checkout we offer. Support animals are welcome.

By the way, if you find that you're getting the same question over and over, you might want to update your listing to answer it there. This saves you time and makes for a better guest experience.

If you're just starting out, you will want to handle all guest communication yourself to get a feel for what guests want and how you can improve your service. As time goes on, you might want to consider some level of **automation**, or **outsourcing responses**. There are companies who specialize in this, and they should be easy enough to find online. I can't recommend any because I've never used any.

No, I've never outsourced guest inquiries or responses. I'm sure the professional outsourcers do their jobs well, but I would still need to stay on top of them, and after all, it's my name out there, my property, my Airbnb status and my bottom line.

I'm not such a huge Airbnb operation that it consumes all my time. If I were spending three or four hours a day on guest inquiries, I would consider automation or outsourcing, but not if I were just starting out. I really enjoy connecting with my Airbnb guests from around the world. From their communication, I have learned a lot of important information about my property, guests and how to improve. This comes from reading every inquiry and every guest communication myself that first year.

The bottom line with response and acceptance rates for me is that I make it a top priority in my day-to-day work operations. I can be surfing at the beach or having lunch at a local cafe and I can easily open up the app on my phone and take a few minutes to answer an inquiry. I have all the saved message templates on my phone, which makes it almost effortless. If I were a guest making inquiries, I would want a property to get back to me within an hour or two, and I can reasonably expect that most of the time. I'd give preferential consideration to properties who seem like they're more interested in serving me than the ones who aren't.

So I'm constantly checking for new inquiries when my listing is accepting them, I regularly update my description if I find guests have questions I'm not answering in the listing, and I simply treat guests the way I'd like to be treated myself.

MARKETING TECHNIQUES

Let me insert a word here about marketing. I'm not going to spend a tremendous amount of time on this, mainly because it's my Airbnb philosophy that the things we've discussed so far, such as presentation, communication, pricing, location and property condition, are what you should focus on. If you do the basics well, I firmly believe that success will follow.

I'm all for clever and effective marketing -- I think I'm pretty good at it myself. But I've seen friends who believe they can cover up flaws in the property with glitzy marketing tricks. They may get some quick bookings this way, but their reviews suffer, and long-term, it has always come back to bite them. I can't think of anyone who's built a successful Airbnb business with exaggerated marketing.

The rule with marketing is that **your marketing must always be behind your property**. In other words, if your marketing is presenting a better promise than your property can deliver, this will result in a poor guest experience and that's a bad marketing strategy. If your property's a 7, your marketing should pitch it as a 6.5, not a 9. If the marketing *slightly* undersells the property, guests will be delighted and reflect that in the reviews, which is much better for you in the long run than, let's face it, fooling people.

There is never any reason or need to misrepresent your property via marketing. Airbnb is too well structured for a property to succeed with that for long. Your marketing must match your property.

That said, marketing is a fun part of the process and there are clever, fun ways you can spice up your Airbnb property's presentation:

Vanity URLs. These catch people's attention -- /swiss-alps-vacation-cabins, for example. The Airbnb Help Center has good advice and information on this, as well as guidelines for what's acceptable and what's not in terms of their content policy.

Area travel websites. Consider listing your property on local tourism or accommodation sites. This may depend on how open your local tourism industry is to Airbnbs in general (some won't list STRs as a matter of policy), but it's worth a shot since many travelers trust these sites when booking accommodations.

Tell your story. Note that I said "your" story, not "a" story. In my Airbnb listing, I mention that this property has some Hollywood movie history. I don't exaggerate what happened, and I certainly don't make up fictional celebrity connections ("Tom Hanks stayed here!"), but I say that there was a moderately significant association here. For some people, that enhances the experience, while for others, it's just gee-whiz information. If there is something about your property that does have an exciting story, find a way to weave it in.

Facebook ads. If you have the means to do so, you can run ads on Facebook because they're good at targeting location. It pays to hit a couple tutorial sites on how to create an effective Facebook ad.

Lifestyle bloggers, influencers. My best advice is to create a collaboration contract that mutually benefits your property listing and the influencer. When you work with a social media influencer with thousands of followers who stays at your property for free, they can be an excellent earned media opportunity for you. For this to be a successful collaboration, you must do reference checks and assess the quality of their previous articles and social media posts to see their level of professionalism in writing, video editing, and photography. If done correctly, this collaboration will be a genuine marketing asset. I have had many successful partnerships where a lifestyle blogger helped a property, especially during the first six months and the slow season.

Search Engine Optimization (SEO) search results. Optimizing your listing using Airbnb SEO is the first step to getting more bookings. You can do this in many ways, and it all relates to communications. These include getting more 5-star reviews, responding to guest messages quickly, updating your calendar, using Instant Book, providing details in your Airbnb profile and updating it with new information, and promoting your profile on social media. If you follow these tips consistently, you will boost your SEO.

Business cards, brochures, flyers, handouts. Some people swear by these. Not everybody learns everything online anymore, so sometimes placing physical paper promotional materials at local restaurants or events brings in business. It doesn't hurt to keep some business cards with you to hand to people who might inquire about the property.

Vacation rental forums can be good places to swap stories or pick up pointers and advice. Talk about your property in Facebook Groups dedicated to vacation rentals in your area. Most of my long-term rentals (one month or more) for my property in Puerto Vallarta, Mexico come from Facebook group inquiries.

Special events and offers. You can run seasonally-appropriate discounts or events for guests (a 15% off Mother's Day or Valentine's Day specials), or offer guests a 10 to 20% discount on future stays, or incentives for referring others to your property. Airbnb has a referral program; you can create one of your own as well. Word of mouth is still one of the most effective means of marketing in any industry, make sure your property gets it for the right reasons.

FIVE-STAR REVIEWS

It's no exaggeration to say five-star reviews are solid gold on Airbnb. There is little that correlates as closely to your profit as your guest satisfaction, and five-star reviews reflect this.

Everybody wants to hear from someone who's experienced a property. Face it, inquirers don't know how accurately your listing, your wonderful photos, etc. reflect the experience they'll actually get at your Airbnb. We've all been burned by slick presentations. But to see a few dozen people say "Five stars! This is a great place!" takes a lot of the hesitation out of booking a property.

So how do we get them?

Be honest.

Nothing is more important. Nothing. See, the great secret of five-star reviews is that *they reflect guest expectations, not objective property quality.* If the guest expects a modest cabin with basic sleeping arrangements, and that's exactly what they get, that's a five-star review because that's what the guest expected to pay for. They didn't expect chocolate mints on the pillow so they don't ding you a star or two for not providing them.

On the other hand, if you have a spectacular property but lead the guest to expect more than what the property can deliver, they will feel cheated. N*o matter how wonderful it actually is,* they won't give you five stars. In a previous life as a customer loyalty consultant, I learned that negative impressions are far more powerful than positive ones, and people are up to 10 times more likely to share negative than positive comments. The #1 most important thing you can do to get five-star reviews is to set guest expectations and exceed them a little. If you wildly exceed guest expectations time after time, you're underselling your property and it's time to update your listing.

Write an accurate listing.

This is the first order of business. Your listing must match the guest experience as close as humanly possible. Spend the time it takes to get flattering yet accurate pictures, and point out all the positives of your property while being fully honest. If there's road noise, mention that. If there's construction, mention that. If things get chilly at night, say so -- tactfully, not "it sure gets cold here, folks" but "enjoy snuggling up to a warm fire with a hot drink in the chilly evenings" -- so they're not unpleasantly surprised.

Protip: When I send guests a follow-up email thanking them for staying, I ask,"How can the property be improved?" Notice I don't ask, "Did the property live up to your expectations?" It's too easy to check "yes" just to be done with it. If everything was fine they'll say that, but you're much more likely to hear suggestions for improvement by avoiding yes/no answer questions. Another activity I do with every new Airbnb listing is to stay in it myself for 3-4 days to ensure it has all the household items required to make a pleasant stay for guests. From the welcome mat at the front door to the kettle and tea selection in the kitchen, I make sure guests have what they need to have a comfortable experience.

Make the location clear.

For some reason, "location" gets more unmerited negative ratings than anything else on Airbnb. No matter how clearly you describe your location, in picture and word, some guests will rate you down for it -- *even when it's exactly what you told them it would be.* If you're in midtown Manhattan, guests will complain about the location's noise. If you're on a farm, they'll say they would have preferred a subway stop close by. There is nothing you can do about this. We all hate this, but you're not alone, friend.

Pretend each guest is your first one.

Act as if THIS guest's review will make or break your business. Find some way to go above and beyond for each one. Remember my chocolate idea.

Welcome them with a note.

It's so easy yet so appreciated. "Hello Chris and Terry, we're so glad you're staying with us!" Read enough guest reviews and you will see lots of them mention the welcome note. Oh, and please double check the names. These attention to detail moments are very important to the guest experience.

Check their previous reviews.

Sure, why not? See what things they complain about or knock properties down a star or two for. Protect yourself by avoiding as much negativity as you can. Read both their reviews of properties and host reviews of the guest.

Use the check in, check up and check out messaging.

Whether you use the Airbnb chat, email or text, contact the guest within 24 hours of their arrival with as much detail as they could reasonably want to know, including your contact information and an invitation to ask any questions. Most of the time, I text and use the Airbnb chat and post the same information just to ensure they receive the message. Many times, guests' text messaging may not work because of data connections, but as soon as they are on wifi they will receive the Airbnb chat message.

Protips: In my **check in** message I write, "Hope you'll have a five-star experience!" Clever, isn't it? **Check up** after they've gotten settled. This is when they can tell you about a missing remote control or a burned-out lightbulb so you can fix it right away and get a five instead of four-star review. When they **check out, thank** them for staying with you and ask about any issues -- the idea is they'll tell you in a private message instead of saving it for the review.

Leave a gift.

Nothing fancy. Fruit, chocolate, a jar of local jam, something. On the topic of chocolate, I am highly in favor of providing some. A mini box of Lindt truffles costs me $1.25 and is always next to my welcome note to guests. The majority of guests love chocolate and this sweet addition helped me boost a basic property I had in the city. I know this because I would get messages from guests after they checkout thanking me for the chocolate, water bottles, Guidebook, tourist guides and welcome note with my favorite restaurant suggestions. Airbnb is known for having better amenities than hotels, so don't let your guest's expectations down. This is a case of "it's the thought that counts," just like with that *Vogue* magazine left for me years ago.

Make a good first impression.

Meet the guest's expectations and exceed them with the little things like the welcome note and the gift, as well as keeping the place as bright and clean as possible.

Pay special attention to children.

If there are children or babies staying, be sure to meet whatever requests you've agreed to. And gifts you leave for children are twice as appreciated as gifts for the parents.

Write a good house manual.

There are articles and templates on writing a top-notch house manual. Read them. A well-constructed house manual heads off more frustration and complaints than you can imagine. Include everything from local restaurant reviews and recommendations to how to work the TV to local transportation information to interesting places to visit in town to how to turn the stove on and off and how much coffee to use per cup. Format it in an easy to scan bullet point style guide.

Explain the importance of Airbnb reviews.

Most guests honestly don't know how important they are. Don't grovel and beg for five-star reviews, but it is appropriate to send a brief text saying how important a good review is to your property's Airbnb success, and how you've tried to think of everything, so if there's anything you've missed please contact you immediately and you'll make it right because you want their stay to be perfect. There will be the rare guest who will ding you for not fixing a problem they refuse to tell you about. This can happen to you, but you can minimize it with proactive and open communication with your guests.

Write your own guest review immediately.

You get to write a guest review as soon as they check out, and they won't see it until they write theirs first. But if they know they have your review waiting, it makes them more likely to write one for you.

Protip: The percentage of guests who leave reviews factors into achieving Superhost status. This is a great, subtle way to remind them to review your property.

Reply to public reviews.

This helps build guest trust. It shows that you listen to guests and take them and their concerns seriously. Either thank the guest for a good review and say you hope to see them back soon or apologize for the guest's poor experience, and outline what steps you've taken to prevent it in the future and invite them back.

ASK YOURSELF

1. Is there any way I could be responding to inquiries more quickly than I do?
2. Looking over the list of ways to improve the number of five-star ratings I get, which ones could I implement?
3. In the ways I market my property, is there anything I'm presenting that's not quite true?

Being a good host will take you very far in your Airbnb business. The focus of true hospitality is serving others, so if you can master that, a world of benefits opens up to you. From word of mouth marketing and five star reviews, one positive guest experience can bring you limitless bookings in the future. In the next chapter, you will learn how to automate your Airbnb business so you can have more time freedom in your everyday life.

CHAPTER 6 - AUTOPILOT MANAGEMENT

> **KEY TAKEAWAY:**
> This chapter gives you ways you can improve your efficiency and find greater time and money savings by automating certain aspects of running an Airbnb. Even the simplest and most basic of hacks can save many Airbnb owners a significant chunk of time and worry.

AUTOMATION, FOR MANY PEOPLE, BRINGS UP NEGATIVE IMAGES--sitting on the phone forever running through a "Press 253 for Swahili," or robots getting our orders wrong, or online "Help" menus that seem to offer anything but the help we're looking for.

So why would anybody running a business like an Airbnb, where success relies so heavily on that personal touch, want to turn it into an automated experience?

Of course you don't want to automate every single thing about your Airbnb; you'll never be able to just sit back and watch the money roll in without lifting a finger. What we're talking about is saving yourself time and mistakes by automating those parts of your business -- don't forget, we are running a business here -- that can be automated with no loss of the quality of customer service.

Here's what I mean. How much time a week or a month do you spend doing the following things:

- Writing and sending the same exact email to guests?
- Driving between key handovers?
- Producing individual reviews for all your guests?
- Researching your competitors' prices and updating yours across all platforms?
- Dealing with support staff like cleaners and contractors, and having to get in touch with them at odd hours?

Automation can greatly cut down, if not eliminate, much of the time you're currently spending on these tasks with no loss of customer service quality, freeing you up for more important things to do with your day.

There are other benefits to automation:

- You're not distracted from the more important aspects of your business that require the most thought and attention. If you're running your Airbnb as a modest side hustle, this is doubly important, since you really want to keep the workload as low as possible.
- The more guest communications are automated, the

faster and more efficiently things happen. Replies get out faster, so bookings tend to go up when guests decide to go with whoever gets back to them first over less responsive Airbnbs.

You can grow your business faster since you're not wasting time on things a computer could be doing for you.

WHAT SHOULD I AUTOMATE?

The basic rule is if it's a repetitive task done regularly and pretty much the same way each time, it's a good candidate for automation. For example, adjusting prices can and should be automated. You can even automate transactional guest communications. But, this does not work for guests who ask for a personal response to a specific issue and get unhelpful automated emails. They will not leave five-star reviews with that type of service.

And this brings up another issue with automation. Your guests expect it. Only the most unreasonable of guests, who are quite rare, thankfully, expect a personally-crafted response or interaction every time they contact you. When you make reservations online, you don't expect the head of the airline to sit down and write, "Hi Anthony, thank you so much for reserving a seat on the Vienna to Cairo flight." Especially if your name's not Anthony.

Guests know you are running a business and they expect you to take advantage of automation for routine tasks in your business workflow where appropriate.

So, how do you go about it?

Guest Communication

Start here. Friend, if you're writing everything from scratch for every guest interaction, we have good news for you: We're about to save you a ton of time -- some studies have found that replying to guests, your current and prospective guests, takes up to 75% of the time running an Airbnb property. You can't totally eliminate that time, but you can minimize it.

Plus, Airbnb takes your response rate pretty seriously when

deciding who gets Superhost status, so don't leave this to chance.

Note that these communications can be sent as emails or text messages, not only through the Airbnb system. It might be a good idea not to rely solely on the Airbnb notification system because guests don't always have it turned on. Sure, it's their fault if they miss a communication from you if they don't, but that still contributes to a negative experience. It's much better just to send redundant messages across platforms to ensure they receive the communications.

Email templates. Solid gold. These get you out of cutting and pasting email responses, or worst of all, hand-crafting new ones. There are plenty of Airbnb templates available online, so find one you like that reflects your personal style and the vibe of your property. If you are a bit tech savvy, create your own personalized templates and use them for a variety of guest interactions:

- **Initial inquiry response.** "Hi, thanks so much for contacting us, we'll get back to you ASAP."
- **Common answers to common questions.** Keep track of the questions you have to answer over and over, and create a template for them.
- **Booking inquiry.** This is for someone who has already contacted you and wants more information about your property before they decide to book.
- **Booking request.** Here's where you accept or reject a request to book your property.
- **Booking confirmation.** "Thank you for deciding to stay with us, we're looking forward to your visit, here's some information you may find helpful…"
- **Check In.** If guests don't request it ahead of time,

about 24 hours before they're scheduled to arrive, send a reminder of their check-in time, directions if appropriate (and for the forms of transportation they're most likely to use), instructions about the key, the Wifi password, anything they'll want to know and have all in one place without extraneous clutter -- do not put restaurant recommendations, etc. on the check in message. Also don't put check out information here except for a reminder of their checkout time and date.

- **Check Up.** Soon after your guest has arrived at the property, you need to check up, asking if all is well: Is there anything they need or anything else you can do for them? This is where you can include an Airbnb Guidebook that has restaurant recommendations and fun things to do in the area. This book contains free additional resources to level up your Airbnb communications. Resources include easy-to-customize templates to use in your Airbnb. Check them out at: www.luckybookpublishing.com/airbnb.
- **Check Out.** Remind them of the procedure for check out, anything involving trash or dishes or whatever else they're responsible for upon leaving.
- **The review request.** Write them a note soon after check out, reminding them that you've written a review of them, you hope they had a five-star (HINT HINT) experience with your property, and you'd appreciate a review from them as well.

"But won't all this sound too impersonal? Won't they think they're dealing with a robot?" No, this is not a concern. Frankly, many people appreciate what is obviously an automated response to routine, frequently-given information, since they know it's free of mistakes.

Automated Sending. In other words, an Airbnb email **autoresponder**. This is the next step after you've got your templates in order. Automation tools catering to the Airbnb market allow you to set a send time, which you can set to 24 hours before check in, one hour after check in, half an hour after check out or whatever suits your own property. If they need to put the trash out Tuesday morning, you can automate an email to remind them of that too.

Automated Apps. If you want, you can create an app guests can download on their phones with all the information they need, such as TV instructions, restaurant recommendations, any manuals or your property policies they should be aware of. About 20% of STR managers offer these, a recent survey found. And you can put personalized messages on them as well, of course.

- Automated apps can save you a lot of time. There are people who swear by them, but personally, I don't use them. I don't like asking guests to do things that are more for my convenience than for their guest experience, and while downloading an app may not seem like a huge ask, it's just one more thing they have to do that they don't really benefit from, and one more thing to remember to do when they'll be checking their email or text messages anyway.

Other Regularly Automated Tasks

Smart locks. These can go a long way toward automating checking in and out. All it requires of your guest is to enter a unique access code. There are no keys to hassle with (for them or you) and no rushing over to open the door for locked-out guests. I use them and find them convenient. Other options are lock boxes, the kind real estate agents use, and they are also an effective way to save time and cut down on mistakes.

Automated pricing. We've gone over what you need to know for basic pricing strategies. There's a lot to remember, a lot of ingredients in the stew -- weekend rates, peak and off-season rates, special occasions throughout the year, length of stay, etc. You can find automation tools created specifically for Airbnb that minimize uncertainty by automatically raising rates for weekend stays, dropping rates when there's too long of a gap between bookings, etc. You can set your own pricing rules and the tool automatically enforces them.

- Dynamic pricing strategies generally give you the best profits on your property, but they can eat up a tremendous amount of your time if you're doing them manually. There are Airbnb pricing automation tools on the market which analyze all the criteria that go into setting prices for STRs, run them through a proprietary algorithm, and come up with what they consider ideal prices every 24 hours.

Cleaning and maintenance. This has got to be one of the most enjoyable aspects of running your own Airbnb, right? Ha. It's a chore. Whether you're doing any cleaning or maintenance work yourself, all of it, or having to track and manage a professional service, it's work, and it takes time. This is especially true when you've hired a local individual to do the cleaning instead of a full-fledged professional service, and they have an emergency and can't complete the schedule for you. There are apps like Properly which list cleaners and maintenance pros in your area with performance reviews. Professional cleaning and maintenance companies are more expensive, so you need to decide for yourself if the peace of mind is worth it when automating your cleaning and maintenance schedules with a preferred vendor.

- This is a good place for a quick word about maintenance best practices: One thing I do is limit the number of breakable things in my property when there's a guest. Hey, if it can be broken, sooner or later it will be. Trust me. I have very sturdy furniture, washable walls, and no glass or delicate ceramic knick knacks or trinkets lying around on coffee tables or shelves when the property is open to guests. It's not that I don't trust their intent; they're not out to break my stuff, but it just happens. Heck, I break my stuff, but I'd much rather it be me than a guest who does because then things get unpleasant and awkward.
- Do you have a maintenance professional and handyperson on speed dial? It's so important to have professionals on your side for when emergencies arise to ensure you are getting the best service at competitive pricing. I learned this the hard way when one of my properties had a broken toilet in the middle of the night and I didn't know a plumber. I had to pay above market prices due to the emergency situation and time of day. Now, I always have a reliable maintenance professional on call.
- Protip: Schedule regular proactive checks on major appliances so there's a minimal chance of having to, say, replace the refrigerator during a guest's stay, or

worse, having the air conditioning or heating conk out at the worst time possible. But when the inevitable happens and there is a maintenance issue, you want to have a good relationship with a local company or individual to handle the problem. Professional property management companies take care of this as part of the service.

Reviews. Yes, you can automate this to a great extent. This is one area I don't automate because I like my guest reviews to be obviously personally tailored, but my Airbnb guest load is nowhere near what it used to be (by my choice), so I have the time for this. You may not, and you may find a tool helping you set up automated guest reviews makes the most sense for your business.

Smart amenities. This is an interesting part of the Airbnb business, and it relates to smart customer relationship management. Your guests expect the basics, sure. It's when you go above and beyond that you're delighting them. Offering free Wifi is not delighting your guests since they would be upset not to have that. Automatically offering a free jacuzzi is delighting your guest – that's not something they necessarily expect.

- A liberal pet policy is also a delight for many guests, but do exercise discretion with this, of course.
- Local specialty food products automatically placed in the room without the guest's specific request, either by the cleaning team, yourself or a property manager, are great ideas too.
- Temperature control capability is also important. There are automated tools, like Nest

(www.store.google.com), to ensure that your property is maintained at a maximum comfort level for your guests.

Concierge service. Again, depending on your business volume and how much time you have, it might make sense to hire a concierge service for your Airbnb. This automates answers to any questions guests may have 24/7. They can be somewhat pricey, but I do know Airbnb owners who couldn't do without them. I've used them at times, particularly during the busy seasons, but I find I simply don't have the need for them year-round.

Hosting automation tools. If you have Airbnb properties listed on multiple platforms, you'll really want to check out hosting automation tools to cut down on confusion and mistakes. Double-bookings are awful experiences for guests, as are missed cleaning jobs. You can find automation tools that do things like manage more than one account and list all on a common dashboard. They can also synchronize calendars, unify email inboxes, work smoothly with automated guest communication templates and autoresponders, track cleaning and maintenance schedules, and process client bookings, invoicing and payments.

- Are these products, many of which are significant financial investments, worth their cost? In general, the more properties you have, yes. And if you're running properties on different platforms, the need for one powerful hosting tool increases substantially. Over time they almost always recoup their investment cost by the number of bad reviews they prevent through organizational simplicity. And as we all know, bad reviews lead to lost income, so anything you can do to eliminate problems before they arise is practically guaranteed to be a smart investment.

In general, **vacation rental software** exists for pretty much any automation you could imagine. Do look through a few vendors' offerings. They'll at least suggest ways you can save time and money by automation, and you might find one that is really worth its cost. I've used some of them, and generally found them helpful when I was running a much bigger Airbnb operation than I am now. Any good vacation rental software product will have a comprehensive suite of messaging features. Make sure one does before you purchase it.

The Check In Process

In addition to guest communications regarding check-in, the process itself can be streamlined by automation.

Certainly start by automating guest communications as much as possible. Create templates and set up an autoresponder. In most cases, you shouldn't have to personally interact with a guest before they arrive, unless they have specific questions you need to answer that are not covered by your templates.

Some form of automated lock system is usually available. There's a lockbox you can buy from your local hardware store. Tell your guests where it is and what the number combination is to open it.

We've already covered smart locks, which are the most secure option currently available. They do require the guest to have a smartphone, which the vast majority of your guests will, and they only work for one access point.

There are also key exchange services. I've heard good things about Keycafe (www.keycafe.com), where guests can pick up keys during business hours.

The Check Out Process

Again, assuming you have guest communications automated, if you want to automate the key retrieval process, or go with smart options, you can save time for the guest. You can automate guest reviews, or do them personally. Either way, be sure you offer guest reviews quickly. Since the guest can't see it until after they review your property, the curiosity factor really helps them remember to rate your property.

I also set an automated follow-up email as part of the check-out process, set for a month or so after they've left. If they've left me a five-star review, I have a template where I thank them, invite them back and offer a 10 percent discount if it's during a slow season. You might find that business travelers are on a yearly travel schedule, so they'll be back in the area that time next year. An automated reminder before they plan their accommodations in a year's time might prove rewarding.

The Cleaning Process

In addition to what's already been said above, bear in mind that usually guests expect professional hotel-standard cleanliness in your property, unless you make it pretty obvious that part of the charm of your property means it's not going to be hospital corners clean. There are rare exceptions where this should be the case.

Most of the time, it does pay to automate cleaning, whether you have a local individual contractor and a couple of names on backup, or a professional service you can set and forget.

Some owners like to do a personal walk-through before guests arrive, and this is my preference. Nothing substitutes for your hands-on quality control guarantee -- after all, it's your name, your property, your reputation and your business.

Other Automation Options

Bulk purchasing. Seems an odd thing to discuss under automation? Maybe, but that's how I think of it: When I buy things like coffee, toothpaste, garbage bags, dishwashing soap and any cleaning or guest products in bulk, not only am I getting lower prices, but I'm also "automatically" supplying these things for future guests. Okay, perhaps it's just my own systematic way of seeing the world, but this saves me as much time, effort, mistakes and hassle as any automation tools or procedures do!

Channel distribution. For certain Airbnb operations, channel distribution is something that makes sense to automate. If you're looking to go beyond Airbnb and get your property listed on multiple channels, you'll need to do more than just sync your calendars. You will be greatly in need of vacation rental software that manages all your varied location listings in one version of the truth, consolidated in one place.

Again, this prevents double bookings, which are just land mines as far as your business goes. You do NOT want to double book guests. Your Airbnb ranking suffers horribly, as does your reputation. I've never done it (knock on wood) and I feel for those who have. So you want to do everything in your power to avoid this, and vacation rental software is a must if you want to go the channel distribution route to promote your property.

Calendar sync. Take the worry, guesswork and manual mistakes out of the realm of possibility with scheduling automation. When you have more than one property listed on Airbnb, ensure that you sync their calendars on the Airbnb site. It's under Listings>Availability>Linked Airbnb Calendars. If you're offering the property on other platforms you can import other calendars into Airbnb that support the iCal format -- Google Calendar, etc. Property management system tools help do this for you.

Hiring staff. This is what "automation" boils down to: having something or someone else do a job for you. It's one thing to set an email autoresponder; you do that once and forget about it. Using a vacation rental tool is another level of automation, and hiring staff is a bit more complex. You can outsource anything and everything about running an Airbnb for the right price, so you have to constantly weigh, given your time and profit goals, whether an operations manager, customer relationship manager, full-fledged property management company or any staff hires are worth it for you.

AUTOMATION STRATEGY

If you haven't noticed by now, there is a service for just about every part of running an Airbnb! If you used all of them, you'd have a hard time finding a profit, so decide what time-consuming aspects of your business you'd most like to be rid of and automate that.

You should be automating your guest communication as much as you can, but beyond that it's pretty much up to you. Do you just really, really hate cleaning? Automate that. Is it impractical for you to be the one to hand over the key and collect it again? It's easy enough to find a suitable automation solution for that.

The bottom line with automation is that it's a tool for you to use when it makes sense for you to do so and it's cost-effective enough to earn its keep.

ASK YOURSELF

1. Am I currently automating as much of my guest communication as is humanly possible?
2. What aspects of running my Airbnb do I either spend too much time on, or really hate doing, to the point where automation makes sense for me?
3. Of everything I'm currently automating, is it all cost-effective?

Automation is really little more than finding ways to save time and money by having machines or other people do things. In the next chapter, you'll see that you don't even need to have your own property for Airbnb.

CHAPTER 7 - AIRBNBING WITHOUT PROPERTY

KEY TAKEAWAY:
This chapter highlights some unconventional ways of making money through Airbnb - yes, there's a lot you can do without actually owning property yourself.

IF YOU DON'T WANT TO OWN PROPERTY, WHICH CAN BE A MAJOR hassle, or can't own property for some reason, or if you simply aren't into the whole idea of hosting, there is still a lot you can do. This chapter will introduce you to some rather unconventional ways of earning an income from Airbnb without having property under your name.

First, we're going to get very comfortable with the concept of rental arbitrage.

RENTAL ARBITRAGE

Does this sound like one of those complicated financial deals where you need an MBA to make sure you're not getting burned? It's actually quite simple.

Rental arbitrage is when you, the host, decide to rent a property from the actual owner, and then you turn around and rent that out as an STR on Airbnb. Simple, really -- you're just adding one more layer of rent in the deal.

This is getting more popular. Property all around the world, particularly in the United States, is getting more difficult to afford. I have friends in Canada who tell horror stories of the high prices of very modest houses in rural towns. Home ownership is getting increasingly out of reach in smaller cities like Ottawa, let alone Vancouver and Toronto.

Rental arbitrage allows people who can't afford to own property outright to profit from the use of property owned by a third party.

Is It For You?

How do you decide if it can work for you? The math isn't hard.

Using round numbers for simplicity's sake, let's say you're in a city where a one-bedroom apartment rents for $1,500 a month. You check the Airbnbs in the city, and find that the average price for a one-night stay is about $200 a night (again, just using round numbers pulled from the air here). If you rented that apartment, you could make back your $2,000 with 10 stays a month. Anything over that is sliding into profit, after your cleaning and other expenses.

So if you can keep that property rented out 80% of the time, 24 days a month at the $200 rate (remember you can nudge that rate up most weekends), you're grossing $4,800 a month, easily covering your expenses and pocketing the rest.

The Advantages of Rental Arbitrage

Ease of entry. The advantage of ease of entry is clear -- you can start making money without a huge capital investment.

Simplicity. Another great advantage of rental arbitrage is its sheer simplicity -- you have one payment a month, to the landlord, who takes care of all the taxes, homeowner fees, maintenance, upkeep, etc. You turn around and rent the place out yourself, covering all the expenses and pocketing all the profits.

Small risk. You're taking a risk, sure, but when all's said and done, not a huge one. The landlord replaces the roof when that needs to be done, and if you're not making the money you expect, hey, you can just walk away when the lease is up.

Quick scaling. If you find you're in a good area, you can ramp up pretty fast by renting additional properties a lot faster than if you have to buy more properties. Likewise, when market conditions go south, you're not on the hook for a lot of white elephants. You just cut your losses and walk away.

Rental Arbitrage vs. Property Management

"That sounds a lot like property management," you say. It's close.

Property management means you're not really in control of the property, you simply take care of it for someone else. The homeowner obviously will take a share of the profits since it's their property, and the homeowner can dictate blackout dates when they will be using the place themselves.

Generally, you have little to no control over that, and frustratingly, blackouts tend to get scheduled during the most desirable times, like when you could be renting it out at higher rates to travelers.

The Drawbacks of Rental Arbitrage

Rental arbitrage works great if you've spotted a good deal in a stable housing market where there's a steady demand for STR properties. It's hard to lose money in a situation like that.

But there are some scenarios where you should think long and hard if rental arbitrage is for you:

Seasonal fluctuation. Just like if you own your property, you're going to have variable spikes and flat lines in demand. When it's your own property, you're not losing as much money during down times as you are when you're paying the same rent every month, whether it's high or low season. Like with any STR, there are going to be ups and downs. Can you still make a decent profit overall when including the down times compared to the rent you're paying for the property?

- And again, as with a property you own, you can try offering discounts and special offer packages to boost occupancy during the slow seasons, but if you're renting someone else's place it's more urgent that you find that income to cover your costs and afford you a decent profit.

Volatile housing market. Are you thinking of setting up your Airbnb in a place where market conditions could fluctuate significantly? If so, will you be locked into an unfavorable contract and ultimately find yourself unable to generate enough revenue to cover the unexpected increases in your fixed cost. i.e. the rent you're paying?

Complexity. Yes, I know I said simplicity was an advantage of rental arbitrage, but the actual lease you sign to get the property is a complicated document (see below). Paying a lawyer to help you here is a sensible investment saving you lots of grief later on. You might even need to get permission from neighbors in certain situations.

It's still your name on the lease. Granted you don't own the property, and Airbnb does offer some protection for guest damage, ultimately it's you who has to ensure that any damage to the property will be fixed. This is the same as if you own the property yourself, of course, but when it's your own property you get to decide when good enough is good enough. A third party landlord might have a different idea of what's required to make them optimized than you do.

Natural disasters. I'm not trying to be the voice of doom here, but yeah, these happen. Is the area you're thinking of known for mudslides? Hurricanes? Earthquakes? Floods? If Mother Nature acts up and tourism dries up in your area for an extended time, can you afford the rent? Do you have a backup plan?

Getting Started

So you've sat down and worked out the pros and cons, asked for advice, prayed, talked to some landlords in your area to get a feel for the stability of the market, meditated, checked out the going Airbnb rates against rental rates, pondered your horoscope, consulted the local laws governing STRs in rental properties, read the tea leaves and you've decided... to tackle rental arbitrage!

You've seen an opportunity, done the math, and you're sure you can make it work.

Great! Let's get started.

The contract. This breaks down into various stages itself:

1. Find the property you want to use for your Airbnb rental arbitrage, contact **the landlord**, and -- I can't overemphasize this enough -- **be honest** and tell him or her exactly what you're doing. Please. If you fudge the issue, telling her "Oh, I might have a couple friends over once in a while," and she finds out you're running an Airbnb -- which she will, guaranteed, 100% -- you could very well be in hot water. Tell the landlord "Hi, I want to rent your apartment to operate it as an Airbnb, I expect ____ guests per month." This should be enough to reassure her that you'll be above-board in your dealings with her.

2. Let her know you've familiarized yourself with the **local laws** covering this situation.

3. Promise to cover any **damages** to her property and not to cause headaches for her with **the neighbors**.

4. The landlord will do due diligence on you, of course: your creditworthiness, references and gut feel. But landlords can't do that with every guest who books your Airbnb. These are the dreaded **unvetted guests.** Landlords fear them. You have

to reassure the landlord that this will not be their headache. To mitigate risk, ask for a security deposit from all guests. You will walk the landlord through Airbnb's screening process. And ultimately, you will reassure her that the buck stops with you on any damage or problems.

5. Airbnb offers some **insurance** for guest damage. Check the site carefully to understand all of its terms and nuances, but it can protect up to a million dollars. Let the landlord know this, as it will be a great reassurance to her. You can also take out short-term rental insurance yourself to convince her further that any and all damage will be taken care of.

6. **Amendments.** You've reached a handshake deal with the landlord; she's clear that you're using it as an Airbnb and she's cool with that. Now it's time to sign a legal lease.

- You agree to pay the **fines** if you are found to be in violation of any local laws or ordinances (now you see why it's important to ascertain whether you're in a stable, established, relatively predictable housing market?)
- You offer the **liability insurance** the landlord is comfortable with, either Airbnb's option or a third-party short term rental insurance policy.
- Some landlords may ask for a **cut of the profits** in addition to the rent. Decide if you can live with this or not. Whatever you decide, get it in writing.
- Some landlords may also want a **reserve security deposit**. This is understandable; lots of guests will mean more wear and tear on the property (especially if you're renting a furnished property). Comply with this request.

7. **Setup.** You've signed a lease with the landlord who knows exactly what's going on with the property. Most properties will come with a fridge, stove and the like, so it's up to you to get it all decked out with everything else a guest expects.

CO-HOSTING

Another option that might work for you is the co-host approach. This is where you partner with someone else's Airbnb property, offering to help them manage the property. It's not technically property management since you're operating more or less in tandem with the property owner, not just as their employee.

A co-host helps prepare the property for the next guests, takes care of guest communications, keeps an eye on the cleaning and maintenance, maybe even creates listings and welcomes the guests -- everything the host would do but doesn't have time for.

Co-hosting is a good way to break into the Airbnb market, to decide if this really is for you. Expect to earn about 20% of the listing price per night, but if you do a significant amount of the work it's not unreasonable to ask for up to 40% of the listing price.

How Do I Become a Co-Host?

There are a few ways:

- **Ask.** Find an Airbnb host you know and ask if you can help out as co-host.
- **Get to know a host.** Stay at a local Airbnb and get to talking with the host. If he doesn't need a co-host right now, he could later, or he might know someone who does need help now.
- **Job boards.** Search for an Airbnb co-host.

AIRBNB CONSULTANT

Another path you could take is to be an Airbnb consultant. I've used them in the past and found them knowledgeable and helpful, well worth their fee.

Generally this appeals to people who have run Airbnbs themselves. Airbnb consultants tend to be former hosts who turn to consulting, not consultants who decide to add Airbnb to their list of services.

The main benefit to being an Airbnb consultant is the same for being most any "consultant" -- you can just set up a website and away you go; you're in business. You don't need credentials or formal licensing. Just set up a website and boom, you're an Airbnb consultant.

You do need a system for gaining clients, establishing a pipeline of new work as you go. Which means you'll need to find Airbnb hosts willing to pay for your expertise and advice.

I know when I hired Airbnb consultants I was looking for someone with a specific skill set in addressing specific problems I was having at the time. I didn't just want anybody. The consultants who could show me that they went deep into the particular areas I needed to improve -- specifically, listing, presenting and targeting my sweet spot guest -- were the ones who got my business.

So how do you do this?

- Be able to **sell yourself.** If you're uncomfortable selling yourself, this gig probably isn't for you. People are not going to beat a path to your door. You will

have to go out and drum up business by convincing people they need you.
- Offer specific **ROI** (Return on Investment). In other words, your pitch isn't "Hire me and I'll improve your Airbnb business." Your pitch is "Hire me to maximize your bookings, improve your listing rankings, increase the percentage of five-star reviews, and attract more targeted guests."
- Figure out your **niche**. What are you really good at -- better than most? Specialists are in greater demand than generalists. Find out what problems Airbnb owners are having by reading Airbnb host blogs and noticing where their business pain points are. Hit a lot of Airbnb consultant sites and see what they specialize in, look at your skills, and figure out what problem you could be solving for people that there's a demand for.

STR PROPERTY MANAGER

As I said earlier, there is a difference between being a co-host and a property manager, but maybe being an STR property manager is more your thing.

What does an Airbnb property manager do? Just as the name suggests, they don't own or host the property. They make life easier for the owner or host. As a property manager, you're a hired hand, and you rarely receive a cut of the profits.

This is good and bad for some people. Many folks just want a steady job without having to worry about their compensation being tied to ups and downs. Other people are drawn more to the excitement of building an Airbnb business.

The downside, of course, is you can expect to be worked pretty hard. The owner will want maximum value for your pay. This often means you're on call, and you're doing the least fun things -- scheduling cleaning and maintenance work (and jumping in when they don't show up and you can't find a replacement), making sure everything with guest communications runs smoothly, troubleshooting problems and emergencies -- whatever the owner can have you doing.

But if you like managing things and want to explore property management, here's how to become an Airbnb property manager:

- Look for **owners looking for a co-host**. Owners who think they want a co-host often actually want a property manager. Watch CoHostMarket (www.cohostmarket.com) and similar sites, Facebook groups, personal networking, or Airbnb hosts you stay with.

- **Sell yourself.** Yep, you're in basically the same position the consultant is -- if you're not selling an Airbnb stay at a property, you're selling yourself. Obviously play up any and all experience you have. If you don't have experience, it's a tough sell, so have reasonable rates starting out. You can raise them once you have a track record.
- Take a **property management course.** Yes, that's a thing, and it's a nice certification to have to reassure potential clients.
- **Write up a business plan.** You're starting a business, after all, even if the business is you. Do your background research on everything the job entails, talk to other property managers and find out what separates the good ones from the not-so-good ones. You'll need to show potential clients that you can handle things like pest control, plumbing, electrical, HVAC and whatever other issues may arise with the property, especially in the context of emergency support.
- Familiarize yourself with the most popular **vacation rental software** options. Just like the owners need to automate as much as possible, if you're going to manage properties you need to maximize your time as well, and you'll be using the same systems the owners will.

Property Manager Qualifications

Here's the good news: You usually don't need formal qualifications to do this. If you're good, if you have a deep knowledge and grasp of the STR industry and you get your foot in the door in a couple places to build a track record, that's all you need.

Some places do require certain licensing to manage STRs. Check your area carefully across all levels of government (local to national).

Yes there are certifications you can get from courses that help you get started, but after a while it's all about your performance. Do a great job and you'll never be out of work.

How much money will you make? It varies greatly -- anywhere from 10 to 50% of the listing prices. The average yearly income for a property manager in the United States is just south of $60,000, according to the latest numbers I've run across. Obviously those starting out bring the average down, while the established, successful ones are making more than that.

AIRBNB CLEANING SERVICE

Here's another way to be involved in the Airbnb industry without owning property. The upside is there's no shortage of work if you're reliable. Hosts usually hire outside cleaners, and you can get started at very low cost.

Again, you need to market yourself and what you bring to the table. There is no substitute for sterling recommendations, so it might pay to work for a professional cleaning service for a year or so to have sufficient experience when you strike out on your own.

Expect to make about what other cleaners in your area make -- frankly there's nothing unique or magical about Airbnb cleaning compared to cleaning any other apartment.

House Sitting

Why are we talking about house sitting on an Airbnb site? Because house sitting is something that has absolutely nothing to do with Airbnb whatsoever.

Nothing. Period.

This is a warning: Do not accept an offer to house sit for someone and then turn it into an Airbnb, figuring you'll make some quick cash by renting out a house you've been entrusted with for free. Not only is it a dishonest thing to do, but if you get hooked on making easy money you'll do it until the inevitable disaster strikes.

If you have a sweet house sitting gig, great. Enjoy the money you're saving and do not use it as an Airbnb on the sly. Airbnb itself frowns on the practice, they will not help or support you in any way if you get in trouble.

Partner with Airbnb

And finally, you could try partnering with Airbnb itself. Their partner program basically pairs you up with local hosts and you help them on predefined roles with whatever they need -- cleaning, hosting, publicity, etc. You set your fees and schedules in negotiation with the hosts. Apply on Airbnb's Local Partners page.

The OMG Fund

Recently, Airbnb sponsored an OMG Fund to invest in some of the weirdest, quirkiest, craziest properties it could find. Some look like hobbit houses, while others look like a giant shoe, a spaceship, the Yellow Submarine, a double-decker bus and the list goes on. Entries are closed now, but let's hope they do this again.

AIRBNB SUPERHOST AMBASSADOR

Here's where you get paid to help new hosts succeed. You are connected by Airbnb to people who would make good hosts, and you help them in any way you can to succeed. You're basically an experienced mentor. Again, apply on the Airbnb Ambassador site.

Influencer

Finally, you could go the influencer (www.afluencer.com) route. With platforms like Afluencer, you can create a profile and specialize in travel and Airbnb reviews. Airbnb also partners with big influencers with lots of followers to sprinkle their magic dust over properties. This is an option if you have 1 million visitors or app hits. If you do, it should be easy to join the program. As an influencer, you can also contact Airbnb hosts directly to see if they would like to collaborate with you.

ASK YOURSELF

1. Do any of these avenues appeal to you more than pursuing the standard Airbnb route?
2. Do any of the unconventional hosting approaches sound like they'll work better than property ownership?
3. Have you really checked out the local market to determine if Airbnb rental arbitrage would be a better option than ownership?

We're almost done. We've gone over pretty much all the basics you need to know to decide if Airbnb is for you, or to improve your results. In the next and final chapter, you'll learn how to protect your Airbnb investment by mitigating possible risks.

CHAPTER 8 - MITIGATE RISKS

KEY TAKEAWAY:
This chapter highlights the risks Airbnb businesses face and how to navigate them.

IF YOU'RE RUNNING AN AIRBNB BUSINESS, YOU'RE FACING RISK. If you're running any business, you're facing risk. Running an Airbnb, your risks include some combination of dishonest clients, an unprofitably low occupancy rate during certain seasons, getting the wrong insurance or insurance provider, breaching local regulations, mishandling security concerns and general safety issues.

Too many entrepreneurs only consider these risks after the negative thing has occurred. Yet it's possible -- and important

-- to mitigate them in advance, saving you and others time, trouble and expense. This chapter will help you.

You can use this chapter as kind of a mega-checklist. Not all of the issues here apply to all Airbnb owners or operators, of course, but you should be able to say "No, that isn't a risk I face," rather than "Gee, I didn't know that was possible."

LEGAL / REGULATORY CONCERNS FOR AIRBNB PROPERTIES

This is something I've tried to emphasize throughout this book: You simply must be aware of the legal status of STRs in your area. Do the work. Research this -- rarely will all the answers be on the surface. You have to dig to make sure nobody can use the law to cause problems for you.

And the fun never stops. Localities, usually at the lower levels of government, are forever tinkering with STR laws and regulations, and you have to keep on top of all of them. Schedule regular reviews to find any legal modifications that affect you.

And you don't stop at just one level of government.

Federal

The federal government of your country usually doesn't get too involved in the details of STRs. There are the usual taxation and reporting requirements, of course, and you really should be consulting with a tax pro about that, particularly since there are almost always ways to deduct expenses and other money-savings which you don't know but a professional does.

Keep all receipts, keep good records, consult with a knowledgeable tax professional, and you should be fine with the national government.

Provisional/State

This level of government does get more involved in the details affecting your Airbnb business. Of course they're keen on taxing you as much as possible as well, and some have laws and regulations for the STR market. Poke around online so you know what questions to ask the authorities to make sure you're in the clear and complying with all state or provincial regulations concerning Airbnbs.

Municipal

Here's where the government really starts paying attention to you. They control the zoning laws that you MUST know well, and business licensing laws which you also must know inside and out. Don't rely on news reports or secondhand "Oh, that's not allowed in this part of town" information from local officials. Ask them to give you chapter and verse of the ordinance. I've been surprised how often local officials themselves don't know off the top of their heads what the law is. You can request they go look it up; it is their job.

And especially if you're just starting out, hiring a legal professional to research municipal, city, township, county laws concerning Airbnb is a great investment to make.

Strata or Homeowner Associations

Here's where you can really get tripped up big time. Homeowner associations (HOA), in my experience, are very concerned about anything that might affect property values, so if you're out of step with their covenants and regulations, they're usually very quick to bring it to your attention. You want to avoid getting on their bad side. There isn't any point trying to fight with an HOA, and in fact they can be very helpful if they sense that you're respecting the neighborhood and their policies. Attend the meetings when you can and get to know the people. If they decide you're good for the neighborhood they'll be supportive of your Airbnb (especially when they have family coming to visit). Personally

I don't have much experience with them, but a friend of mine said her HOA went to bat for her with the local zoning board, which was an immense help.

So you've ensured that your Airbnb complies with the national, state, municipal or neighborhood regulations. Congratulations. There are several other areas of potential risk you need to have informed policies on.

Security Deposits

A fundamental way of mitigating risk. Of course, you should be collecting one from every booking no matter what. Standard policy, no exceptions. No guest worth having is offended when they are asked to provide a security deposit. It actually shows that the Airbnb business owner takes pride in their property and wants the protection.

That said, as I've mentioned earlier, be hesitant to deduct expenses from it. I mean, it has to be really outside the normal cost of doing business. If the guest breaks a cheap drinking glass or coffee mug, you don't buy a new set and charge it to the security deposit. If the guest breaks Waterford crystal, you smack yourself for having had it in the property in the first place and negotiate a replacement path with the guest. We once had a guest who dented the wall with a small hole and stained the carpet. They informed us in advance of the damage and we used the security deposit for repair costs.

How big should the deposit be? A standard figure is around $250 USD. Guests will find that reasonable. It's up to you if your particular property merits a higher or lower one.

Guest Vetting

Let's face it, if someone is going to cause you risk, it's almost always going to be a guest. How do you vet guests to be as certain as it's possible to be in this crazy world that a guest is not going to cause you any grief? There are steps you can take to vet potential bookings before opening your property to them.

- **Their Airbnb profile.** The more complete it is, the better. The more verifications there are, the better. Read the "About Me" section and see if anything throws up a red flag -- their age? Interests? General maturity level?
- **ID verification.** Look for the "ID Verified" badge on their Airbnb account.
- **Airbnb reviews.** Pay very close attention to these. Yes the vast majority are going to be positive, but there are ways of deducing potential issues by how they're worded, reading between the lines -- "Extremely high-spirited, fun-loving, vivacious guest!" could mean "Party animal." Be warned.
- **Social media.** If you can find and access their Facebook, LinkedIn, or other social media presences, do so. You don't have to scour every possible source, but you should be able to get a general idea pretty quickly if this is a person you want in your property or not.
- **A quick interview.** Sure, you have every right to do this. Ask them: What brings you to town? What did you like about my particular listing? Will you be alone or will there be someone staying with you? What will you be doing while you're here? Done

right, it will come across as professional and friendly, not the third degree of police interrogation. Be sure you get full names and contact details for everybody on the reservation.
- The **Vacation Rental Agreement.** When you have them sign it, make sure it contains your expectations of guest behavior, the house rules and guidelines as well as your property's cancellation policy and all payment information.

What not to do:

- Do not discriminate based on a guest's race, color, ethnicity, national origin, religion, sexual orientation, gender identity or marital status. Airbnb prohibits this. Read their Anti-Discrimination Policy carefully. You do not want to be caught discriminating, even innocently and unknowingly.

INSURANCE

The first thing to do with insurance is familiarize yourself with what **Airbnb** offers you in the way of protection. They can cover you up to a million dollars for property damage and even bodily injury, but check the terms carefully. You don't need to hire someone to do this for you the way you should with government regulations. Airbnb does a good job of making it all clear and plain on the site, just allow yourself enough time to read it all and make sure you understand.

It's been my experience that what Airbnb has is good in its way, but it's not enough for true peace of mind. You will almost certainly be better off taking out coverage that isn't as limited as what Airbnb offers. **Short-term rental insurance** policies are easy to obtain, and much more suited to your practical everyday needs. Sit down with an insurance agent who can clearly explain the different policy tradeoffs. You do not want to leave this to your own efforts unless you have a pretty strong background in the insurance industry.

Given the specifics of your Airbnb operations, you might need **business insurance**. I've never had the need for a great deal of coverage here, but I know STR owners who do and it's a sensible expense. It might be for you, too. Ask the agent who's explaining STR insurance to you if taking out an additional business insurance policy would be a benefit. They'll say yes since that's how they make their money, but based on how they explain it you'll be able to tell for yourself if you really need it or not. The key consideration here is how strictly local laws define your renting out your property as a business.

You do need specific STR insurance no matter what other coverage you have.

Locks

Door locks are the big thing here, and they're not as boring as you might think. Smart locks are increasingly popular with Airbnb owners (as well as with the general public at large). The technology is quite advanced these days, you can install ones that not only record and notify you whenever the door is opened, but also tell you how many times someone goes in or out, and if it's currently locked or if the guest forgot to lock up.

Some smart locks have the capability to allow you to remotely restrict access, setting strict check-in and check-out times, and preventing guests from returning after they've checked out.

Cameras

Do not use indoor cameras at your property if you have Airbnb guests staying. Period. This is a huge violation of Airbnb policy, and you will most likely face stiff legal action from righteously angry guests as well. Exterior cameras obviously intended for property security are acceptable, but just make it clear to the guests where they are and that they are in use.

Noise

This is a sensitive area for some people. You can install noise monitors for security, ensuring no wild parties are taking place which will either damage your property or annoy the neighbors, some of whom could make life quite difficult for you. But some guests don't like feeling that their conversations are being recorded, or that they even could be. You can explain that the noise monitor you use only records decibel levels, not actual conversations, but if they're uncomfortable with even that it's your call whether or not to insist on it or remove the device during their stay. Generally you can get a gut feel for whether noise will be a problem with a booking or not.

Along with noise prevention, it's perfectly acceptable for you to write guest ground rules for your property that the guest must agree to. They should be worded tactfully, as this isn't a lecture you're giving your sixteen-year old before you go out of town for the weekend.

Maintenance

You might not think of maintenance as a risk issue, and maybe technically it isn't, but it does affect the security deposit in some ways. It's never a bad time to talk about how to save time and money, so here are some ideas for minimizing property damage risks by preventive maintenance:

- Have furniture that is both sturdy and easily cleanable.
- Make sure you have the appropriate number of smoke detectors and that they're all in good repair with charged batteries.
- It could be a good idea to clearly label all exits if it doesn't clash with the decor too much. By all means, point them out to guests upon arrival, either in person or with a welcome note.
- Look after the towels and linen. Make sure they're hotel grade and are replaced a little earlier than

necessary, as opposed to just after their shelf life expires.
- Dark fabrics are much easier to clean.
- Feel free to ban or allow smoking as you wish.
- Don't let maintenance issues rise to the level of risk; take care of problems when they're small, when you first notice them.
- Keep good track of all warranties for all your items and pay attention to expected life dates.

General Risk Reduction

Here's where I put all the good advice I've accumulated here and there over the years:

- Always go with your gut instinct on whether or not you can trust a booking. If it's a group of young men, don't automatically assume it's a stag party. It could be a spiritual retreat or brainstorming session. If you're genuinely unsure about a possible booking, either decline it -- better safe than sorry -- or ask for a larger security deposit. Or, if it's feasible, ask for a personal interview, especially if it's your home you're renting out, and particularly if you'll be there as well.
- If you get a last-minute booking from a local resident, that is a big red flag. I'm not saying to decline the booking automatically. I'm saying to make sure you know what's up with that. It might be that somebody showed up at the last minute and the person genuinely can't accommodate them. Check these people's references carefully.
- Don't get lazy about checking guest reviews for new bookings. This is an essential risk mitigation step in

your Airbnb business. And be honest when writing your guest reviews. If there are genuine reasons why hosts should beware of someone, let them know. You'd want them to be honest about people booking your property, so pay the honesty forward and good karma will reward you.
- Be crystal clear about whether or not you're required to collect tax on your guests. This goes under the general awareness of laws and regulations above, but ask this as a specific question when you sit down with a tax professional. I speak from experience.
- Smart locks are the way to go.
- No doubt you're aware of valuable items that could be stolen and you've taken measures, but also be certain that there isn't anything on the property that would allow a guest to commit identity theft. A great idea is one from the old Travis McGee novels by John D. MacDonald -- McGee was something of a private eye who lived on a houseboat. He hired a professional thief to try to find where McGee had hidden his money. If the thief did, McGee knew another thief could as well. You don't (necessarily) need to hire a genuine criminal, but find someone with the ability to conduct a search of your house to make sure they couldn't commit identity theft if they wanted to.

LOW SEASON RISKS

This is as good a place as any to remind you of the most fundamental risk you take when you get in this Airbnb business: the slow season. It's going to happen; there's death, taxes, and Airbnb slow season, but there are things you can do to make the best of the slow season.

Pricing. Lower your price during the slow season to catch what business there is out there. Less profit is better than no profit. Some industry observers recommend lowering prices as much as 90 days in advance of what you know is going to be a slow season.

Prepare for busy times. Farmers use winter to repair equipment and prepare for the next planting season. Use the slow season for large-scale maintenance and property improvements.

Airbnb of Event Space. Companies such as Peerspace (www.peerspace.com) and Splacer (www.splacer.co) rent space for events, meetings, photo shoots, etc. Nobody spends the night at your place; they use it in the daytime. It might not be for everybody, but it's worth at least looking into.

Renting Your Home for a Film Shoot. Movies will pay to use your home in a film. This can be lucrative - renting at $2,000 to $3,000 a day as locations, and the rates have been known to climb as high as $25,000 a day. They will also cover expenses such as your hotel fees and incidentals per day. Just be very careful to understand the scope of the film shoot, as this option comes with its own risks if the script calls for explosions or natural disasters.

Adjust availability. Instead of just booking three to six months out, try opening it up to accept bookings a year in advance. You might cash in on some people wanting to plan long-range.

Be a "Discount" property. Throwing "10% Discount" into your listing title itself will perk up some eyes. If someone's already decided you're within their budget, seeing an extra 10% off is an impressive little surprise. You can also add Seniors and Veterans discount to your listing description.

Reduce the nightly rate. Then reduce it again. Seriously. Hotels sometimes lower their rates as much as 40% in the off season. How low are you able to go to attract business? You can even reduce it below the minimum break-even rate because something is better than nothing at the end of the year. Renting out a room at a $20 loss is better than standing firm on principle and getting $0 for it.

Increase your discount. Then increase it again. This works best for long-term guests.

Eliminate the extra guest charge. It's really not all that much more costly to you to have an extra person in there. I've already discussed the economic pros and cons of the extra person charge. But there's really no defensible rationale for it during the slow season when you're just happy any warm body is in the place. If there is some genuine economic reason why you have to charge it, lower it during the slow season, or get rid of a charge for the third or fourth person -- "Fourth Person Stays Free" promotions actually catch some eyes.

Rethink your Airbnb pricing strategy. You know, the one you have automatically set. Feel free to manually adjust it during the slow season.

Improve your listing. Now why don't more people think of this? There are two ways to increase business during slow seasons: either lower the price or raise the attractiveness of the product. If you're already operating at pretty much rock-bottom, to the bone prices, you can gussy up the listing to be more appealing.

- This would be a good time to see if you can get better quality photos on your listing, or improve the captions to give the reader a clearer, more compelling experience.
- Rewrite parts of the listing to appeal to the kind of person who would be traveling during the slow season.
- Are all your accessibility features up to date? Has anything else changed about the property recently that would make it more attractive?
- Take stock of any recent notable changes or improvements in your area and make sure your listing is updated to account for them. We're talking about *anything* that could possibly interest a guest.

Go all-out on customer service when you do get a guest. Give impossibly wonderful service to get a glowing five-star review and great word of mouth.

You have **verified your ID**, right? Good.

Try InstantBook. If you've never tried it, the slow season is the best time to experiment. Some people feel that guests like InstantBook better. It does make some parts of trip planning easier, that's true. Your response rate is faster so you get more of the impulse purchase crowd's bookings, and during the slow season it's good to take any advantage you can get.

Change the minimum stay. If you have a minimum stay policy, you're probably already increasing the number of nights in the required minimum stay during peak season. That's good pricing. Now lower them during the slow season.

Get the major cleaning done. Housewashing, cleaning behind the refrigerator, checking the linens to see what needs replacing – slow season is a good time to catch your breath, deep clean and take inventory so you're ready to hit the ground running for busy season again.

Reduce the extra fees. If you charge a cleaning fee, for instance, which I don't recommend doing in the first place, you should get rid of it during the slow season. We've already discussed doing away with the iffy extra guest fee. Be sure if you do so that you make a point of advertising it.

ASK YOURSELF

1. You do know there will be a slow season. Are you ready for it?
2. Have you done all the legal and insurance legwork to ensure you're as protected as you can possibly be?
3. Are you doing anything that contravenes any of Airbnb's operating policies, such as the anti-discrimination guidelines?

You can never be perfectly safe; a life devoid of risk is a sad one, but you can be as safe as reasonably possible.

CLOSING

So there you have it, friends: my advice, wit and wisdom to help you become an Airbnb Superhost and, if it's your goal, to replace the 9-5 routine and join the new rich. If your goal is just to make some money on the side, or if you have a day job you really like, this book should point the way for you to do that as well. Either way, done right, Airbnb is an incredible journey.

I've enjoyed writing this book. It's brought back a lot of great memories and some more "interesting" learning experiences. But that's the thing about Airbnb! Dealing with people, especially the kind of people adventurous enough to travel around with Airbnb, is endlessly interesting. I've made genuine lifelong friends from some of my guests; I've visited them and stayed in their homes (for no charge!)

If there is one way to sum up everything, the Airbnb secret of success, the secret sauce to becoming a Superhost, achieving your financial and freedom goals, it would be to see everything from your guest's point of view, and be what you would want a host to be if you were in their shoes. Know the law, know the local regulations, have a plan to tide yourself over the slow season, stay cool with your neighbors, don't sweat the small stuff and focus on the big picture. Learn as you go and don't lose faith.

If you have any questions or would like to connect after reading this book you can get in touch with me at:

hello@luckybookpublishing.com and

www.luckybookpublishing.com/airbnb.

Do well and have fun!

RESOURCES

Abraham, S. (2022, March 11). *5 Ways to Value a Real Estate Rental Property*. Investopedia. https://www.investopedia.com/articles/mortgages-real-estate/11/how-to-value-real-estate-rental.asp#toc-2-the-capital-asset-pricing-model

Abualzolof, P. (2016, September 24). *Airbnb Reviews: Top Influencers Affecting Your Occupancy Rate*. Mashvisor. https://www.mashvisor.com/blog/airbnb-reviews-influencers-affecting-occupancy-rate/

Airbnb Titles: Proven Formulas That Attract 5x More Bookings [Examples Included]. (2020, April 27). iGMS. https://www.igms.com/airbnb-titles/#4_Proven_Formulas_for_the_Best_Airbnb_Titles

Carl, A. (2021) *Short-Term Rental, Long-Term Wealth*. BiggerPockets Publishing.

Deane, S. (2022, January 4). *2022 Airbnb Statistics: Usage, Demographics, and Revenue Growth.* Stratos. https://www.stratosjets.com/blog/airbnb-statistics/

AUTHORS NOTE

Thank you for reading Airbnb Investing 101.

It is my deep desire to help you achieve the Airbnb hosting success you envision.

I hope Airbnb Investing 101 has taken you one significant step closer to just that.

I would like to ask a small favor of you. No obligation whatsoever. Would you be willing to post an honest review of Airbnb Investing 101?

I ask because reviews are the most effective way for fellow entrepreneurs and investors to discover the book and determine if it will be of value to them. A review from you, even a single sentence or two, will achieve just that. To do it, simply go to the website (or the website for the store) where you bought the book and submit the review.

Again, I seek only your honest feedback. If you loved Airbnb Investing 101 please say so. If you have suggestions for the book, please share that too.

What matters most is that other investors hear your truth about Airbnb Investing 101.

Thank you. I am wishing you your most successful Airbnb investing year yet! Abundance and success are yours!

James

BONUS CONTENT: CHECKLISTS AND TEMPLATES

Attention to details is essential in running an Airbnb business. This bonus content of checklists and templates are included to help you level up your properties and save you time and money. Not to mention, they will show your guests how much you care and rise you to the top of Superhost status.

What You Will Receive

Easy to customize templates to use in your Airbnb. No design experience needed. All you need is a free Canva account.

- Guidebook
- Welcome Sign
- Wifi Sign
- Instagram Sign
- Check Out Checklist Sign
- Cleaning Checklist
- Essential Items Checklist

Go here now to get your additional resources included with the book. Enjoy!

www.luckybookpublishing.com/airbnb

Printed in Great Britain
by Amazon